NCE Exam Prep

2019-2020

A Study Guide with 300+ Test Questions and Answers for the National Counselor Exam

Table of Contents

Introduction 7

Notice **8**

Chapter 1 – A Background of the NCE Exam 9

The Need of the Test 9

Competency... 9

Chapter 2 – Test Sections, How the Questions are Arranged, and the Format.......10

The Eight Main Sections of the Test 10

In Which Sections Do People Do Well? 13

Pilot Questions 132

Layout of Questions 14

Another Way to Understand the Topics..154

Chapter 3 – The Five Areas of Work.. **165**

Chapter 4 – Segments of Counseling.. 17

Chapter 5 – The Test Administration Process **19**

Applying to Write the Test 19

Details of the Test... 210

Computer or Written?.. 210

Recent Changes to the Tes 210

What to Do if You Fail the Test 221

Accommodating Special Needs? 221

Chapter 6 – Human Growth and Development **242**

The Concept of Development.. 242

How Changes Are Viewed 22

Self-Concept 23

Developmental Concepts.. 22

Ways of Learning 25

Neurological Aspects 26

Other Theories 26

Chapter 7 – Diversity 27

The RESPECTFUL Cube 27

Identifying the Client's Needs 27

Chapter 8 – Relationships 29

The General Process 29

Helping Qualities 29

Listening 320

Posing Questions 33

Reflections 33

Explaining Concerns 34

General Guidelines For Responding 32

General Counseling 36

Chapter 9 – Group Counseling 35

Norms 35

How Similar? 35

Engagement 35

Chapter 10 – Career Development 36

Super's Career Development Theory 36

Holland's Typology 36

Personality 37

What About Testing? 38

Chapter 11 – Assessment 39

Free or Forced Choices? 39

Self-Reporting 39

Validity 39

A Critical Note 40

Chapter 12 – Research and Program Evaluation **41**

The General Process 41

Key Principles 42

Chapter 13 – Orientation and Ethics **44**

Six Key Principles 44

Ethics 44

Sample Test #1 .... **47**

Human Growth and Development 47

Social and Cultural Diversity 54

Helping Relationships 59

Group Work 75

Career Development **84**

Assessment 91

Research and Program Evaluation **100**

Orientation and Ethics **107**

Test #2 .... **121**

Human Growth 121

Social and Cultural Diversity **127**

Helping Relationships 132

Group Work 149

Career Development 156

Assessment 165

Research and Program Evaluation 174

Orientation and Ethics 180

Conclusion **194**

Introduction

A counselor helps people understand what they may require for their routines and lives and to recognize the behaviors they need to engage in if they wish to move forward in their lives and be better people. In order to qualify and be certified, counselors are required to complete certain studies at a college or university and to pass all the requisite exams.

More importantly, you will need to complete the NCE test in order to practice as a counselor. As a counselor, you may provide services to students, couples, and recovering addicts.

This guide is a review of the information you will need to complete the National Counselor Examination for Licensure and Certification. The NCE test is administered by the National Board for Certified Counselors or NBCC, the main certification body for counselors in the United States.

The NCE test is a thorough and comprehensive analysis in identifying the skills and concepts required to be a certified counselor. The testing process has been used since the 1980s as a standard for identifying the best people who are qualified to act as counselors. Tens of thousands of counselors have been certified through the NCE test since the standard was introduced.

There are two separate tests in this guide each having 160 multiple-choice questions. The tests encompass the eight subject areas of study. Answers are also included at the end of the book with a detailed explanation of each answer.

The questions in this guide are not guaranteed to be part of the actual NCE test but are representative of the type of questions on the NCE tests. The guide also details strategies to use to complete the test successfully.

Notice

The information in this book is intended to identify how the NCE certification exam is constructed and may not be reflective of the actual NCE test you will encounter in order to be certified.

The segments of this book are based on the official test structure that has been determined to be appropriate for use by the National Board for Certified Counselors. There is the potential for the NBCC to change the layout of the test from the existing eight units, although it is unclear as to whether such a change would occur. You can visit the NBCC website at nbcc.org for updated information on the test, as well as where you can take the test and how the test is to be completed.

Chapter 1 – A Background of the NCE Exam

This guide will help you identify what you need to know in order to complete the NCE exam. The National Counselor Exam is a test required for certification as a counselor. The NCE test is approved by the National Board for Certified Counselors. The exam has been in existence since the 1980s and has been used by the NBCC to identify the skills and aptitude of potential counselors.

More than 40,000 people have received certification by successfully completing the NCE exam.

The Need for the Test

There are two reasons why people are required to complete the NCE exam. First, there is a need to receive proper certification in order to practice as a counselor. People with the NCC designation are often preferred by clients. Some employers choose only to hire counselors who have attained the NCC standard.

Second, there is a requirement for a state counselor licensure in order to work as a counselor in one's state. Check with the rules surrounding your particular state to determine the rules for your state.

Competency

The NCE exam focuses on competency. The general content focuses on what the NBCC has determined to be the most important aspects to qualify to work as a counselor. These are based on eight segments prescribed by the Council for Accreditation of Counseling and Related Educational Programs or CACREP. The eight segments are paired with the five work behaviors deemed to be the most important for students to complete. There are separate chapters in this guide devoted to these segments.

The questions are designed with enough details surrounding the ideas that a counselor will encounter in practice. The chapters in this guide will cover the information to answer the questions correctly.

Chapter 2 – Test Sections, How the Questions are Arranged, and the Format

Your NCE test covers eight sections that are vital to know and understand in order to successfully complete the test. There are a set number of questions for each section. The sections are designed to produce a thorough approach to gauging your knowledge of the counseling field.

The Eight Sections of the Test

The eight sections of the NCE test will be covered randomly by the questions. The random layout of questions ensures that you will be challenged during the test. The number of questions that you will be asked will be consistent for each of the eight sections. There are also 40 pretest questions but will not count as part of the actual test.

Each of the sections is based on the standards prescribed by the Council for Accreditation of Counseling and Related Educational Programs (CACREP) standards.

Here's a look at the eight main segments that the test will cover:

1. Human Growth and Development (12)

The human growth and development segment focuses on the needs that people have throughout their lives. You will study how people evolve and how their mental capacities may change over time. You may deal with how children behave and function versus the behaviors of adults. You will learn what might inhibit the development of a person's mental growth. You may also study topics relating to abnormal behavior.

2. Social and Cultural Diversity (11)

Social and cultural diversity refers to how people handle topics relating to the interaction with minorities or people who come from unique situations or countries.

This segment concentrates on cultural foundations of various ethnic people. The cultures of people from around the world are unique and they make up our society. You will learn and understand how many clients function based on their attitudes and beliefs. This portion of the NCE test is designed to help you prepare to work in an environment that is becoming increasingly diverse.

3. Promoting Relationships (36)

The largest segment of the test covers ways to assist people with their relationships. Many people seek counseling when it comes to resolving concerns surrounding their relationships. These include problems involved in marriages, relationships between parents or employers, and other concerns involved with living a healthy life with other people. In many cases, a person might need help with understanding some of the reasons that relationships fail and what can be done to repair relationships and move forward.

The relationship segment also includes how to consult. You will identify how to successfully communicate with a client. You will learn how to recognize a situation and what strategies to use to analyze the concerns or worries of a client.

You will learn the theories and methods involved with helping relationships and the many techniques that can be used according to what is appropriate for managing certain situations. You will also learn to recognize how a person might respond to certain ideas and suggestions.

Family therapy is also be included in this part of the test. Family therapy relates to how well people in the same family are relating to one another. However, the term "family" is not even mentioned in many of the questions in the test as the definition of "family" has changed over the years.

Consultation is also included. Consultation involves how to interact with people and how to make a conversation move forward.

4. Group Work (16)

Many of the counseling situations you will encounter will be group work. The people in many groups might have distinct concerns surrounding how they are getting along with each other.

The group work segment focuses on reviewing how to interact with groups of people. You can use this segment to help you understand the many concepts involved in group work. It requires you to recognize the roles that people play when interacting with each other and how people act, react and think in distinct groups.

The dynamics of how a group works may also be explored – the theories and techniques. The group sessions you will be expected to conduct may include various dynamics of members interacting with one another in various ways and what they might do when confronted with many important details or concepts.

5. Career Development (20)

Career development covers certain theories and concepts surrounding how to advance a person's career what to consider when entering into the professional field. It also discusses how people should behave in a work environment and the everyday aspects that involve your profession.

6. Assessment (20)

It is necessary to ensure the assessment process is handled with care and that you consider what your client might be thinking and how they are acting.

The assessment section of this exam focuses on how to analyze the needs that people have, whether as individuals, family members, or people in group settings. The questions are designed to recognize how competent you are in counseling people and treat people. Some of the materials you can use for analysis have very specific rules or standards.

7. Research and Program Evaluation (16)

Some of the tasks you will complete as a counselor may entail extensive forms of research. These include studies of how people might interact with one another and how they're going to handle different activities. You will be expected to also look at how certain types of people are more likely to engage in certain behaviors than others.

The research world is exciting regardless of whether you're starting a research program or you're participating in one. This segment of the NCE test will concentrate on the things that may develop when you're involved in a research program.

General research assessment standards will also be incorporated in this section. This is different from the assessment segment in that the focus is more on the results of a test rather than the individual analysis of a single person or group. The standards dictate how data is to managed and the results.

The questions in this section will be about the workings of research. This includes understanding what is involved in keeping your tests arranged and your content organized and ready for use.

8. Professional Orientation and Ethical Practice (29)

The last part of the NCE test will entail professionalism when operating in a professional environment. A counselor has to be professional and useful for a client to hire and trust. This segment in the NCE test focuses on recognizing what you have to do to enhance your ability to serve people ethically and with care.

Standards for solutions and the credentials that you require are included in this section. You will also review the roles involved with the orientation process, how a business is organized, and where you can find the help you require in any situation.

The referral processes are reviewed as well as advocacy standards and triage services. General supervision procedures to monitor a client are explored in this section.

All eight of these sections are critical to your success. The NCE test does not organize these questions by section. Rather, the questions are chosen random across all eight sections.

In What Sections Do People Do Well?

There are no "easy" or "hard" parts of the NCE test. You might come across some segments that you could do a little better with than others, but that may be based on the field of study you are in.

The National Board for Certified Counselors analyzed details of the NCE test for 2016 to see how the students who completed the test performed. A little more than 2,500 people who completed the test were analyzed based on their scores. The review found that people often get about two-thirds of the questions correct.

For instance, the Human Growth and Development section achieved an average of 8.51 correct out of 12. The Relationships section had 25.15 correct out of 36. The Research and Program Evaluation achieved 9.58 out of 16, which was the most significant change from the norm.

Pilot Questions

Some of the questions that you are going to encounter on the NCE test are pilot questions. These questions are designed to determine how well a test might be conducted in the future. There is no way to tell which questions in the NCE test are the pilot ones and which are not. However, these are critical to helping keep the data accountable.

There are 40 pilot questions throughout the test. These questions are designed to identify how the test can be improved in the future.

The good news is these pilot questions will not be considered as part of your score on the test. You should still continue to use the same test-taking standards for each question as there is no way for you to know which questions are pilot ones and which are not.

The 40 pilot questions will be in addition to the 160 that you are required to answer during the testing process. Therefore, you might have to answer more questions in one subject than what you expect. Instead of answering 20 questions in the assessment section, you might be required to answer 23 questions, for example. However, you will only be graded for the 20 questions that were deemed to be the official questions. Again, you are not going to be able to tell which questions are the pilot ones. You should not try to analyze these questions too much when thinking about what is and what is not a pilot question.

Layout of Questions

All of the questions in the NCE test are multiple-choice questions. You will have four options for each question.

There are three particular types of questions in the test:

1. Recall

The recall question focuses on recalling some ideas and information you encountered in your studies. Counselors often prefer these questions as they don't require as much effort to answer.

For instance, you might come across a question where you will be asked to identify a technique or standard that should be used in a certain situation. You will be tasked with recalling information and details about the content of your studies.

2. Application

The second question style is the applicable standard. In this case, you might be given a hypothetical situation where you have to decide might work best. You can use the application involved to determine a specific theory or technique that may be used to solve or handle a situation. You may be required to consider ethics involved in solving or giving advice in certain situations.

3. Analytical

The questions that require analyzing situations may need more time to consider the correct answer. You will need to review the principles and other ideas that are involved in the question. You have the option to write down notes surrounding the questions when you complete the test by computer.

Part of working with an analytical question is determining how complicated the question is. You might have to review the quality of the question based on how detailed or involved it is. You should determine the relevant ideas to decide how you answer the questions.

Another Way to Understand the Topics

You can also consider the three types of questions that are based on foundations, context, and practice.

1. Foundations

The foundations include historic concepts, models of value, and any instrumentation that may be used. The foundations are points that all people in the counseling world are to properly work with. You'll have to recognize how the background relating to your field affects the work you are expected to do as part of your profession.

2. Context

The context relates to the ways you can handle the impacts of certain events or how you can identify concerns certain people have and how each case or issue is unique in some way or another.

3. Practice

Having the knowledge that you have accrued so that you can put it into practice is important to your success. You can plan interviews, assessments, testing processes, and strategies to use to directly interact with clients.

Chapter 3 – Five Areas of Work

In addition to being asked various questions in the NCE test surrounding eight particular domains, you will also have to answer questions that relate to particular areas of work behavior. The NCE test includes five work behaviors and there are a number of questions for each one.

1. Fundamental Counseling Issues (32)

The fundamental counseling issues that you will encounter will require you to review the client's history and the concerns that they have.

You may require the information in this segment to help people with many disorders that are impacting their lives. These include people who have disorders relating to anxiety and depression as well as people who have significant personality issues that are influencing their lives or any neurocognitive concerns that you may discover as a result of interviewing and testing.

2. Counseling Process (45)

The counseling segment focuses on identifying how well a person is able to work with a client. This includes how you're going to review a patient. You may use diagnostic processes and interviews. Distance counseling based on written or oral reports that you receive from other practitioners may also be used in your assessment of a client. Other questions will focus on the care of seniors who might require extra assistance or students who are in school. These questions are particularly important for those who wish to be community social workers or wish to work in school environments and serve the needs of younger persons.

3. Diagnostic and Assessment Services (25)

The diagnostic segment relates to assessing a client. This includes looking at how well that person is capable of managing various thoughts and refrain from self harming or harming others. You will need to consider your skills surrounding initial assessments and evaluations to identify how well a person is functioning mentally.

You can use diagnostic and assessment services to identify many aspects surrounding how people behave. Be advised that this segment is not to be confused with other practices surrounding physical concerns that a patient has. Working with a physician may be recommended.

4. Professional Practice (38)

The professional practice segment includes understanding how you are going to arrange counseling events and how you will manage an intervention. It also includes how to schedule a series of sessions for counseling based on what a client might require. You can also work with many counseling models in this segment with each model being based on different cultural aspects that you may encounter.

5. Professional Development, Supervision, and Consultation (20)

The field of counseling is always evolving and that there will be many ways how you're going to change and evolve in your work. This point will focus on how you will continue to grow your practice and how you will communicate with others who might work with you or for you in the same office situation.

Part of this segment also involves communicating with people who prescribe medications or with others who work for professional organizations that might assist you in understanding the client's need for medications and the reasons medications were prescribed.

One more point to note about these work behavior areas is that there is no particular section that is harder than another. The segments are only as hard as you let them be, as you would have to complete enough studying throughout your work to ensure you have a better chance at handling all of the questions that you will encounter in the test. In most cases, on average, people achieve 60 to 70% of the questions right in each section.

It is expected you might come across many job opportunities as a counselor. The comprehensive nature of the NCE test ensures that you'll work to acquire many skills covering all the segments involved.

Chapter 4 – Segments of Counseling

An essential part of the NCE test is devoted to working in specific segments of counseling. All counselors can find work based on their specialties. This chapter will help you understand the different forms of counseling that will be covered in the test.

1. Addiction Counseling

Addiction counseling deals with people who are experiencing addictions. Counseling is given to those who are experiencing problems at work and at home due to their addictions. The client needs support to find healthy ways of coping with their struggles in life. Counseling should consider mental and physical wellness, cultural concepts, and how other psychological disorders may be prevalent in the life of the addicted client. People who are addicted to various drugs or alcohol items might be ones who might not be able to correct their addictions on their own. Ethics is an important element for you to consider. For example, who should be privy to client information and how do you protect the confidentiality of information?

2. Career Counseling

Many of the best counselors help people understand their career choices. You can use the NCE test to identify how to manage different ways to build a positive career and make an impact on the lives of others. Your work in this area should entail many analytical points relating to roles and settings that people might work in. Reviews of the needs an individual has and the skills that a person possesses are deciding factors of a career choice. You can also review questions in the NCE test surrounding different ways to direct people to job opportunities.

3. Clinical Mental Health Counseling

Clinical mental health relates to counseling clients who are suffering from mental health issues. Particular mental functions might be influenced by various factors. Cultural factors can influence how people handle and perceive mental health. You should focus on questions surrounding clinical mental health if you are going to work with people who have mental disorders to help them manage their lives and behave and act in society.

4. Clinical Rehabilitation Counseling

While the first segment listed in this chapter relates to handling people who have addictions, this part of the test involves how to handle those who are rehabilitating from any addictions that they have overcome. You can review questions involving clinical rehabilitation to discover the multiple ways rehabilitation services can be provided to former addicts. These include methods such as independent living or halfway home settings. General case management standards can be covered as well.

5. Counseling College Students

Many counselors are employed on college campuses. These counselors help identify the developmental needs that young adults might have. You should note the questions surrounding college counselors and how they can manage trauma or crises and concerns that suggest a person is at an elevated risk of experiencing mental health issues. Many college counselors may also help people find jobs in various fields.

6. Marriage and Family Counseling

There are many intricacies that go into married couples and families. The relationships between multiple people can be complicated. Those who are not on firm ground might be in jeopardy of struggling to get along with one another. You will come across many questions in the NCE test surrounding how couples and families communicate with one another or have a breakdown in communication that causes a severe upset. The NCE questions surrounding marriage and family include some questions dealing with the roles within a family and how the members interact with one another. Events outside of the home can impact a relationship within a family as well.

7. School Counseling

The NCE test has questions regarding how children are to be cared for and supported. You will encounter many questions involving how a child can develop in a healthy way and what concepts must be explored when addressing issues of a child. Many questions relating to school counseling can also give you insight into what you can do in the event you have to refer a child to another type of professional who might offer services to handle more severe cases.

The good news is that many of these questions can include details that carry over to any specialty you might want to focus on. There are many options to consider, so look carefully at the content in a question and how it might relate to your field of interest.

Chapter 5 – The Test Administration Process

This chapter focuses on many aspects that relate to how the test administration process works and what you can expect. Knowing about the administration process helps to identify many things surrounding the content and how the data is laid out.

You must ensure you know the right time and center to write the test.

Applying to Write the Test

1. Decide which type of test you want to complete.

Ensure you have completed the appropriate educational standards to enter the field of study you have chosen. Visit the NBCC website at nbcc.org for details of the particular test you want to write. This includes registering for an exam for board certification or to be licensed in the state you want to work in.

2. List details of your education.

You must provide the details of your prior education. The standards include achieving a degree in counseling or another related field. The degree must be from an accredited college or university. You will be required to submit a certified college transcript to confirm the details surrounding your degree.

3. Review the times set for the test.

The NBCC offers various times throughout the year for people to register to complete the test. The exam schedule offered by the NBCC includes different times in every month.

4. Review the charges associated with applying for the test.

The national test charges should be consistent.

The general fee for taking the NCE test for national certification is $195. There is a different fee if you are applying for the test for local state licensing.

5. Review the other rules for your state.

There might be different standards for licensing based in the state you live in or where you want to be licensed. These include other tests that might be required. These tests might be related to the NCE test, although there is no guarantee that every test will cover the same content.

Details of the Test

The test is multiple choice and has 200 questions with four possible choices. Remember that only 160 of these questions are going to be graded and the other 40 are the pilot questions used to identify the types of questions that future tests will include.

It will take about four hours for you to complete the test.

The test usually starts at nine in the morning local time. However, check with the testing center for details.

In the written test, you have the option to skip questions if you need to. The computer version lets you bookmark questions that you can return to later if time permits.

Computer or Written?

The test will either be a written or computer format depending on where you take the test. A computerized form of the test has proven to be more effective in recent time. You are allowed to use a notepad when taking the computer test.

A written test allows you to write directly on the questions.

The rules for the testing process can vary based on where you take the test. Be prepared for either version of the test.

Recent Changes to the Test

There have been a few changes to the test that should be noted. These changes have been made over the years according to the NBCC's standards and ideas of what the test should include. When taking the test for the first time, you naturally will not notice the changes.

1. Questions are arranged with no divisions involved.

Older versions of the NCE test used to be divided into the eight individual sections. In recent times, the NCE test has been adjusted so that the divisions have been eliminated. The questions for each section are scattered throughout the test.

2. Family content is not prominent.

Older NCE tests also included many questions about family foundations. However, the use of family content is no longer as important to the test. This is because there are many definitions of family and family situations. As a result, the family content in the original version of the NCE test has been almost eliminated to keep the questions more realistic for today's times.

3. How scores are reported have changed.

Raw scores were once recorded and calculated based on a pass or fail score.

The scores were determined based on a general curve. It used to be that you could achieve a passing score with 85 to 105. However, the standard for passing varies based on the state you are in. Contact your local state's advisory board for counseling to determine what has been set as a passing score.

4. The question formats have changed in recent times.

The questions have changed over time to focus on not only identification but also how data is applied in various situations.

5. New standards have been incorporated in the test.

Many of the standards for counseling have changed. These include content that has changed, such as diagnosing patients, managing disaster relief concerns, and counseling against self-harm.

What to Do If You Fail the Test

You might end up failing it the first time around. Fortunately, you will be given another chance to complete the test.

You are allowed to retake the NCE exam three times in a two-year period. It is recommended that you study further before you attempt the test again.

You will have to complete the registration process again. You will have to provide a certified college transcript and the same fee for taking the test. You will have to schedule a new time to complete the test. The process of retaking the test can be frustrating, but it is necessary to go through the process to ensure you'll move forward with your studies.

The test will not be the same questions as NBCC uses an extensive database. This is a major part of why the NBCC includes pilot questions on all tests. The NBCC is looking to get as much information on test questions as possible to ensure questions are not repeated.

Accommodating Special Needs

Special needs are considered such as needing added time due to difficulties with mobility or needing a reader to help if you have restricted sight or have other vision difficulties. You'll need to ensure you can get the proper accommodations that you might require.

Talk with the test-taking center for details about accommodating your special needs to ensure you receive the support you require. You should also include a request in writing for assistance when you apply for the test including anyone who has to accompany you.

Chapter 6 – Human Growth and Development

The first segment of the test involves human growth and development. The ideas in this segment focus on the ways people might grow and thrive.

The Concept of Development

Development may be defined as a series of changes that occur within the individual throughout their life. These include changes in not only the physical body but also in the cognitive thought processes and the social development of that person.

Development may be identified through various theories - learning theories of processing information, cognitive theories of belief systems, psychoanalytical theories developed by Freud and others in the field.

A humanistic approach may also be used. In humanism, human beings are considered as a whole and cannot be reduced to smaller components. Human beings are aware of who they are and what they can do with their lives. In particular, humanism will focus more on conscious thoughts rather than what happens in the unconscious mind.

There are several stages of human development. These include stages that are more prominent during certain times in one's growth.

1. Prenatal (from conception to birth)

2. Infancy (from birth to 2 years)

3. Toddler (2-3 years)

4. Early childhood (3-5 years)

5. Middle childhood (6-12 years)

6. Adolescence (13-19 years)

7. Young adulthood (20-30 years)

8. Middle adulthood (31-60 years)

9. Late adulthood (61-75)

10. Elderly period (75 years and onward)

How Changes Are Viewed

The changes that one experiences in life can be divided up in many ways:

1. Qualitative

A qualitative change in the way one develops can be analyzed as a change in one's organization. This may include the development of several thoughts or ideas. The most common form of qualitative change is sexual development which will include new ways of thinking and viewing the world while managing one's mental processes in ways that one might not have considered in the past.

2. Quantitative

Quantitative changes may include a change in one's intellectual development. The ability of the mind to process and use ideas may expand, thus improving upon one's ability to plan and understand consequences.

3. Continuous

Continuous changes are going to appear over time in life. A personality might develop with unique qualities. The complex nature of how personalities develop should be analyzed based on the entire developmental process.

4. Discontinuous

A discontinuous approach to counseling is recognizing changes that are easy to separate from other changes. For instance, you might analyze how one's language skills develop separately from other changes or you might also look at the sexual development of a person.

5. Mechanistic

A mechanistic approach involves behaviors being reduced to distinct elements. You may look at instinct and how a person uses it to figure out ideas. This includes reflexive behaviors.

6. Organismic

Organismic content involves cognition. You might notice a person's cognitive development and ethical development. This is the ability to think rationally and decide on actions that are right or wrong according to society's norms – in other words, what constitutes acceptable behavior and what is unacceptable behavior.

Self-Concept

Self-concept is an idea relating to one's perception of one's own qualities and attributes. The general developments in one's self-concept are vital to the evolution of the mind and how well a person can work within a society.

Self-concept starts developing from birth. An infant has no sense of self. But this will change in the first few months of life. Eventually, the child will develop a sense of self-recognition at around 24 months. The child may be able to distinguish the difference between the self and others. Eventually, the child can describe the inner properties of self at around eight years of age.

The self-concepts evolve with age, eventually becoming more abstract during adolescence. The self-concept becomes stable and the child will begin to notice many positive qualities in their being. One's self-concept may be influenced by one's family and the culture in which he is born and raised.

Developmental Concepts

The developmental concepts you may come across as a counselor will include ideas that will directly influence the ways in which one's mind might change throughout life.

1. Nature vs. Nurture

Nature is genetic factors that one is born with. Nurture is about the care that a person receives and the outside influences that affect one's growth and development. The nurturing effects can be challenging and hard to predict.

2. Genotype vs Phenotype

Genotypes are the genetic features of the individual. These are passed on from prior members of one's family. Phenotypes are the characteristics that are expressed through the genotypes. The behaviors and physical qualities of the body may be determined by the phenotypes that evolve.

3. Tabula Rasa

John Locke argues that all people begin as a blank slate or tabula rasa. A person will develop according to their experiences in life. You can analyze a patient based on their prior experiences to understand why someone might behave in certain ways.

4. Plasticity

The ability of a person to move through different stages in one's life is also known as plasticity. In this case, a person's mind might evolve in many ways. A person will move from one home or profession to another and find ways to evolve and may have or not have developed ways to accommodate changes.

5. Resiliency

There are often times when a person's life may be severely disrupted. Resiliency is the ability to endure the changes that occur in life. It is through resiliency that a person might be capable of managing certain problems or concern so they can move forward and be more positive.

Ways of Learning

People learn in various ways. The ways people might grow are important to notice based on how well certain things might develop in their minds.

1. Conditioning

Conditioning is learning by repeated exposure to a stimulus. People start to learn new things based on what they have been exposed to and how ideas are presented to them. Certain triggers might influence a person to behave in a certain way. Think about the theories explained by Pavlov, Watson, and Wolpe.

2. Operant Conditioning

Operant conditioning is a concept developed by Skinner who believed learning occurs when the person has control over one's environment. There should be a reinforcement of some kind for certain behaviors and these can be positive or negative rewards.

3. Social Learning

Social learning is a practice explained by Bandura. A person's confidence in one's ability to complete a task can influence the ability of someone to learn. This is a point that is inspired by one's self-efficacy. The observation and imitation of behaviors result in social learning.

4. Conflicts

Dollard and Miller argue that the evolution of one's mind entails the conflicts in which participates or which affects them. A person might try to avoid something based on a prior event or may want to have exposure to it depending on whether they found similar events pleasing or if they should be avoided.

5. Cognitive Development

A person's cognitive development was explained by Piaget and involves how a person's mental functions may evolve and develop. In particular, a person will learn complicated concepts according to age. A young child will develop a sensorimotor approach to learning, which will evolve into an operational form as they mature. The child moves on from identifying water to comparing forms of water to understanding very specific ideas surrounding water, for instance.

Cognition includes the production of memory, both short and long-term memory. These forms of memory are not to be confused with sensory memory, which is only retained for a few seconds, although the distinct details may be recalled after a while.

Vygotsky also stated that cognitive development may work in a social context. Those who are exposed to certain social stimuli will develop cognitively differently than those who are exposed to different social stimuli. The ability to learn and how a person learns is dependent on the social stimuli they are exposed to.

Neurological Aspects

The neurological considerations of how a person develops may be considered, although this is not a necessity for counselors to look into. Neurology refers to the cellular functions of the brain and how it evolves. Part of this entails examining neurotransmitters and how they develop and change over time. These neurotransmitters are responsible for controlling brain functions and in producing emotions and psychological reactions. Messages are moved between neurons within the brain, thus stimulating functions.

You'll need to notice the impairments that might be observable due to the neurological developments. These changes might impact how the mind develops.

Other Theories

The NCE test may include questions about the different theories of development. Such theories are Freud's psychosexual theory of development, Erikson's theory of eight stages of development, Piaget's cognitive theory of development, the attachment theory of Bowlby, and the social learning theory of Bandura.

You will also need to consider the links between physical and psychological growth. While you might assume that a person is going to experience much of one's growth in the early years of life, there are other times when significant growth is possible.

Chapter 7 – Diversity

The world is becoming more complicated than ever before. As a result, it is critical for people to understand the many types of people they will encounter in life. Diversity training can make a true difference when it comes to one's general ability to understand the many people that one might be working with.

The RESPECTFUL Cube

The RESPECTFUL counseling cube is a vital aspect of the diversity training that you should have. The cube is a matrix that entails many aspects relating to understanding your clients.

1. Religion

2. Economic class

3. Sexual identity

4. Psychological functionality

5. Ethnic background

6. Chronological stage of development

7. Trauma

8. Family history

9. Unique physical qualities

10. Location

Each of these ten points in the RESPECTFUL counseling cube relates to what you should consider when counseling clients. Some people may come from backgrounds that are different from what you are used to. Others might have gone through unique experiences. Knowing how a person has evolved and developed is critical for your success in communication.

Identifying the Client's Needs

The RESPECTFUL cube is used to remind you to recognize the different aspects of a person's life and have a better understanding of their concerns.

1. Exploring

You have to probe into a person's history based on the RESPECTFUL cube. Do not directly ask questions of the client. Rather, allow the patient to talk with you. You can understand the needs that someone holds when that person talks with you about what they have been experiencing.

2. Understanding

To understand a client's problems, you have to be given information about their relationships. You can work with a better sense of understanding when you look at how someone functions and what that person's background might be.

3. Acting

Acting is deciding how to counsel a client and what advice you can give once you have learned about them and their problems. You will notice when working on the acting process that the person you are counseling has many standards for how life is to work and what one might be capable of managing in one's life.

Chapter 8 – Relationships

The most important part of the NCE test and the part that has the most questions will focus on relationships.

The General Process

A vital aspect of managing the relationships in your counseling work entails looking at the basic process that goes into counseling people. There are several steps that are involved in the effort of counseling.

1. Opening: At this point, you are introducing yourself and getting used to the person you are talking with. The effort is to establish a sense of trust.

2. Exploring: You must listen to the person you are counseling. Listening helps you to identify many things about that person and will reveal their concerns.

3. Understanding: Understanding is being able to clarify what that someone is saying and reflecting upon those concerns.

4. Deciding: After you consider what your client has told you, you'll have to make a decision about a plan to give advice and decide if your client is ready to accept advice.

5. Exploring: You will need to explore the problem based on the intervention you plan on using. You can identify what someone might be thinking at a time and how hard it might be for them to accept an intervention.

6. Helping: You are helping a person to contemplate unique solutions for how they can move forward. You can offer suggestions to resolve their problems and steps they can follow to achieve one of their goals, but they will have to decide if they are willing to implement them.

7. Monitoring: Your client must be regularly monitored to see if they are realizing positive changes in their life. If something is not working, you can offer other solutions for your client to try.

Helping Qualities

Accomplishing a good relationship with your client is essential for your client to trust in your judgment and be willing to try different solutions to their problems. Respecting your client will build trust and will foster a mutual understanding.

The most important thing to do is to express empathy for your client. You have to show that you recognize the worries and problems they are experiencing. It is especially vital to notice that every person has a unique point of view. Empathy can help you identify many points surrounding the concerns that one has. Empathy is being open-minded and is committed to fully understanding the needs of your client.

Empathy is different from sympathy in that empathy is about seeing the world through another person's eyes. Sympathy is about feeling the emotions of what someone is going through. While sympathy helps you to understand the feelings someone has, that is not going to go as deep as empathy. You have to show empathy to illustrate the concern you have for your client and that you are comfortable with what they might be thinking or feeling.

Listening

Much of what you will do when helping someone with relationships will require sincere listening. You have to listen to the concerns that people have with one another while also establishing a better link between yourself and your client. In many cases, the process of talking to someone who is willing to listen is often the first stage in the healing process. This includes looking at the positivity involved with moving forward and feeling more confident in what one wishes to do at a time.

1. Active Listening

Active listening is listening to other people while searching for meaning. You are actively hearing someone and expressing empathy. Body language is important to notice while they are talking. The best way to describe active listening is that it has five stages:

- Listening with your body by leaning towards the client to show you are paying attention

- Using empathy to listen with your heart

- Listening actively with your ears to identify the key points the speaker is making

- Watch for the body language of the speaker

- Refrain from making comments. Only do so when you wish to clarify and things said

The effort you put into active listening will show that you care about your client. Even then, you have to be cautious when engaging in active listening. You have to avoid preparing your response when actively listening. Trying to produce a response might be hard due to the frustration involved. You should also avoid having biases about your client or what they are expressing.

2. Verbal Listening

Verbal listening is making brief verbal responses that show you are listening. You are not going to interrupt the speaker. Rather, you are letting the person know that you care and that you understand what that person might be doing. The verbal listening process is all about showing to the client that you understand what they are talking about.

3. Non-Verbal Listening

Non-verbal listening involves looking at the person who is talking to you. This includes making eye contact needed for interaction. You also have to give the impression that you are relaxed while paying attention and this will make the client more willing to speak honestly.

Posing Questions

You will have to consider how you're posing questions to your client if you want to make the most out of your counseling sessions. These questions should be asked based on what information the client is giving and what you feel needs to be done to move forward.

You have to consider asking these particular questions:

1. Open Questions

With open questions, there are no wrong answers. You can ask a person anything relating to specific bits of information or ideas. You can ask open-ended questions to make it easier for people to feel comfortable when talking with you. The effort can help you to start the conversation and allowing the client to keep on talking.

2. Closed Questions

Closed questions are ones that can be answered with either a yes or no answer or with a brief answer. Closed questions can actually stifle a client and make it more difficult for them to continue talking.

Reflections

Reflections are vital to consider when you're speaking with a client about their relationships. It is necessary to look at how you're reflecting the feelings someone has while also affirming what someone is saying.

You have to focus on the feelings that the client has when reflecting on those things. Don't think about what was said. Instead, think more about what they might be feeling and how their attitude about something was formed.

Restating or rephrasing things can also help, as this shows that you are paying attention to what someone is saying. You must not directly recite what someone said in the conversation. Rather, you have to talk with that person about the feelings and the attitudes one has conveyed. Knowing how to talk with someone about specific feelings can be vital to your success when counseling a client.

The affirmation that you provide in the reflection process may also help identify many positives involved in a situation. An effort should be made to keep the suggestions to the client sensible while allowing the person who is talking with you to understand many ideas you wish to share. You have to affirm the things people say so they will feel comfortable with what they are doing and how they are conveying their feelings to you. You can encourage your client to make positive changes. However, the most important thing about affirmations is that you are not judging the other person in the relationship.

Summarizing will also draw the key points that your client was trying to convey and make them clear. As you summarize, you will start to notice connections in what the client is saying. You can use these details to help you clarify details with your client.

Explaining Concerns

The key part of creating a good relationship is to have some sensible ideas that can help. There are many considerations when offering solutions. Useful suggestions may be provided to clients to help them identify many opportunities about what they can do to improve their situation. This includes possibly finding ways to discard or rectify any issues one has.

The suggestions and ideas that you provide have to be supportive. You cannot be overly judgmental over what people are doing. Rather, you have to show a strong sense of interest and understanding.

You can also look at understanding the problem and suggesting options for people to work with. You have to set goals and find a plan of action that your client can agree to try. You will have to monitor and review what your client wants to do and if it is going to meet their goal.

As for the goals you establish together, they need to be suitable for the task at hand. You can keep these goals sensible, but it helps to consider short-term goals initially. Larger goals can be agreed upon that you feel are appropriate for the task at hand.

General Guidelines For Responding

You will have to consider how you are going to respond to a client if you want to make your work together to be successful.

1. Never be judgmental.

A client might say that he or she hates someone. Instead of saying that this is an extreme response, you should ask why they feel that way and what it is they find bothersome. You can use this to create a congenial atmosphere and to get an idea of what someone is thinking.

2. Never inflict your morals.

A person might tell you that he or she does not believe in a particular god. Instead of saying that there is a god, you can ask why that person feels this way, or when they started having this belief. You are not to be judgmental here. You are only asking the client to explain themselves further.

3. Be willing to empathize.

Showing sympathy for someone only means that you're too emotionally involved. Empathy is showing a sense of understanding of what someone might be feeling.

4. Help the client to find their own solution.

A great relationship develops when you're not forcing a client to think a certain way and follow your suggestions blindly. Rather, you can offer suggestions but allow your client to work towards finding a useful solution. You should give the client the freedom to explore ideas and concepts without forcing compliance.

5. Focus on the positive things in your conversation.

There are plenty of positives worth discussion when consulting someone. You have to talk about these positives if you want to make the work you are putting in sensible and attractive. You can talk to your client about anything they want to discuss. You can explain that it takes courage to discuss certain things and circumstances.

6. Never show a sense of shock.

There might be times when someone tells you alarming things like being violent to others or possibly using drugs. You should never express shock when you hear these things. Rather, you need to ask about why these things are happening and what is causing these issues to develop. If there are concerns about self-harming or harming others, you will have to refer the client to someone who is qualified to handle such situations.

7. Never make promises.

You should avoid trying to make promises when listening to things people are telling you. You might say that there are ways to make changes but not all of them will work for you. Never promise that one solution is going to meet with success.

Being hostile or judgmental will make it hard for people to trust you. It could happen that you are not willing to work with someone or they refuse to attend your sessions any longer. Being able to communicate well with someone and not being rough in the process is vital for the best results when reaching someone and talking with that person who needs help from you.

General Counseling

The types of counseling can be very complicated and hard to predict outcomes due to how extensive counseling work might be. In many cases, you might be focused on behaviors, but there are many other aspects to consider.

Counseling often entails a cognitive approach. You would consider the rationales that people have for their behaviors. This includes reviewing what might trigger certain actions or how entrenched some of these ideas might be. How was the behavior learned and what might have caused the behavior?.

Sometimes the very specific trigger of behavior can be determined. This point is more relevant to dialectical behavior therapy, although it could also work as a standard for anything else you want to review. But, it is critical to control one's emotions and not let it influence how you respond to or engage with the client. The proper support, in this case, is essential to counsel the client effectively.

Rational emotive behavior therapy or REBT if often used by counselors to discover what is keeping a person from thinking rationally. You will need to look at the beliefs, affects, and disputes the client has reported when looking at events and how they affect the client. You can also use multimodal therapy to identify concerns involved with what someone is experiencing based on deficits in a client's abilities, how drugs or other biological functions might influence their mind and ability to think rationally.

You could also consider transference. Transference refers to conveying feelings and thoughts to someone. The effort will assist in releasing information on what one might be thinking or fearing at a time. This method may help with controlling behaviors that might potentially become destructive.

Counseling can work with many activities from music to art to dance. You can use various forms of media or other sources to gauge the concerns that someone has or any behavioral issues that might have surfaced in the treatment process.

Chapter 9 – Group Counseling

Group therapy is a process where you are counseling multiple persons who have similar concerns. You have to understand how well people are going to speak with each other and work together to ensure the task of counseling remains uncomplicated.

The best way to explain group work is more than helping many people at once. Rather, it resolves social disorders in many ways. This includes identifying problems surrounding how people in society act and why they might struggle with certain behaviors and ideas. Knowing how to encourage many people to recognize society's norms or ideas to conform closer to those norms is important.

Norms

A norm is the implicit standards of behaviors for people in groups to follow. A norm can dictate what people believe is appropriate behavior and attitude.

Norms can be identified when you listen to people express themselves and explain the behaviors and the problems these behaviors have caused.

How Similar?

There are two types of groups that you might have when working with multiple clients. First, there is a homogenous group. The people in this group have similar characteristics, beliefs, or demographics. The second is the heterogeneous group. This group of individuals has varied backgrounds, behaviors, and beliefs.

Some groups may be open-ended in nature. These are groups that can have people coming in and leaving that group at any time. There are no rules about how often people might join these groups or rules that specify how long individuals must remain part of the group.

Engagement

The engagement rates of certain groups can be complicated and it is difficult to predict who in the group will refrain from participating. Some individuals may dominate the discussions and it is the counselor's job to curtail some discussions and encourage the non-participants to take part by asking specific questions. Some loose rules may be used in some groups.

Chapter 10 – Career Development

You could look at many factors relating to how your career might grow. There are also some theories that may be considered in the analysis process. You could use the points in the career development segment of the NCE test to identify many ideas for developing your career in counseling.

Super's Career Development Theory

Donald Super states that the development of a career will occur over the course of one's life. The extensive variety of your work will vary based on your age and where you practice:

1. Growth (up to 15 years). At this point, you are looking at how the working world works. This includes understanding how many interesting concepts have developed.

2. Exploratory (15 to 24 years). This time frame features making plans for and considering a career goal. This is the time that you would be entering or be in college.

3. Establishment (25 to 44 years). This should be around the time when you have decided on a career, have found employment and can develop the skills you acquired in college.

4. Maintenance (45 to 64 years). The maintenance stage includes reviewing the skills you have developed and deciding if you need or want more training.

5. Decline (65 years onward). You are at the stage of contemplating retirement plan for a life in the future.

Holland's Typology

Holland uses six distinct personality types to identify what one wishes to do and how someone might be more likely to work with specific tasks.

1. Realistic

Realistic personality is considering and accepting the physical work that is difficult to do. This person may not have strong interpersonal skills. People who work in physical labor fields often are this part of the typology.

2. Investigative

The investigative personality takes an intellectual approach to work. A person wants to get answers to questions. This does not mean that someone is going to interact well with others. Rather, that person will think more about the structures and systems of the job. People in the sciences are often likely to be included in the investigative field.

3. Artistic

People who are artistic in nature enjoy expressing themselves. They are more creative in the things that they do. People who work as painters, musicians, and others who focus on creating new things may be people are considered artistic.

4. Social

A social personality is willing to interact and communicate with others are often in the social segment. In many cases, counselors are technical people who interact socially, although a combination of other factors might also be included.

5. Enterprising

People who are more enterprising in nature are ones who are interested in being leaders. These are extroverted people who want to take control of situations and persuade others to follow.

6. Conventional

Conventional attitudes and standards include those who are influenced by an ordered structure that is simple and consistent. A conventional person might be someone who works with numbers like an accountant. Any disruptions in what is happening at any time might be bothersome to these people.

Personality

A person's personality is important when considering a career. You should analyze your personality to see what careers you would most likely be suited to pursue.

Congruence is a unique concept to notice when it comes to one's personality and job choice. Congruence is a reference to how a person's personality type will match the work environment one wishes to enter. This is according to the work of Holland. A person will need to meet a sense of congruence to make a job more enjoyable.

Some events in the workplace or in one's life might influence one's personality to where those feelings are brought into the work environment. Constructs, according to Kelly, can be theories that develop based on the events one experiences in life. Some of the changes taking place in one's life can be frustrating for some people. Sometimes these constructs dictate the activities one is contemplating.

What is also important to note is that there are times when a person might change their goals during the study process. A crypto changer is someone who will change their life structure while maintaining many things in their career. An example of this might be a woman who is starting a family while she is working hard to develop her career.

What About Testing?

There are tests in the career development field that may help to identify details of different careers and what people could benefit from the most.

1. Personality

A personality test identifies the characteristics of a person. The test will review a person's personality to determine the attitudes one has and if that person is compatible with particular jobs.

2. Achievement

Achievement tests identify how well a person can complete tasks. An achievement test looks at the skills a person has and how easy it will be for that person to move forward with certain tasks. Their knowledge and skills will determine how they can manage certain jobs.

3. Interest

Every person has unique skills that might make it easier for a person to perform certain jobs. An interest test identifies how well someone can manage a job based on factors like what types of things a person prefers to do or what attitudes a person has towards particular ideas. The results of an interest test will be specific.

4. Aptitude

An aptitude test will show what kind of job you would be most suited for and is linked to interest as well as knowledge and skills.

Chapter 11 – Assessment

Every client you see is going to respond to your suggestions or processes in different ways. The assessment will help you note how the client is communicating with you and if they are responding in a positive way to your suggestions. The assessment will tell you if you need to employ other strategies or not.

Free or Forced Choices?

Counseling often uses open and closed questions. Free and forced choices may occur in the assessment process. Allowing a client to write an open-ended short answer is a free choice. A forced choice occurs when you give your client a choice of a limited number of answers.

Self-Reporting

You can use different rules for how people can report their answers to help people feel comfortable. In some cases, you can use self-reporting. This is a practice that allows people to answer questions as they see fit. People may choose to answer questions so that they feel is safe.

Self-reporting could be appealing in that it allows people to answer questions on their own terms. However, clients may not always tell the truth. They might feel uncomfortable with what they are saying or thinking, thus making it harder for the counselor and the client to move forward with the counseling services that are effective.

Validity

The validity refers to the degree the test measures what it is intended to measure. The validity is extremely specific. Consider a few types of validity based on the work you are planning.

1. Face

Face validity relates to when something looks like it is valid. For instance, a math equation can be reviewed with face validity. Math entails a rigid series of standards for determining the correct answers. Face validity confirms that the equations being used are valid in appearance.

2. Content

Content validity is a process where a measurement in the assessment process has items that can be gathered from the other sources. In one case, a group of professors may work together to produce a unique test that covers critical content and specific details on which they both agreed.

    3. Predictive

A predictive test will involve the prediction of certain behaviors that will develop later. The predictions will be confirmed later based on the behaviors that are exhibited.

    4. Concurrent

A concurrent test involves a review of certain behaviors or actions that are compared with other tests or behaviors. You might conduct an aptitude test of some people in a class and then compare the results with their test grades. You can use this to identify any patterns surrounding how people learn.

A Critical Note

As important as the assessment process is, you must not assume that the results of the tests you conduct are the results that you might be looking for. There are times when a single test is not reflective of one's full knowledge. A test should be interpreted as only one source of data.

You can consider conducting many assessments of your clients throughout their sessions with you. Multiple assessment reports can help you identify how people are functioning and responding to educational endeavors. You can use these assessments in many ways to enhance how your content works and to determine what people are learning and to get a more comprehensive idea of how people are functioning and working.

You might consider using one assessment at the beginning of your relationship with a client. A similar review can be conducted after a few sessions and again well into the client-counseling process.

Chapter 12 – Research and Program Evaluation

Many counselors will participate in special research programs. These are programs designed with the intention of reviewing concepts surrounding the field of counseling. You might potentially participate in a research study that can help identify new concepts in counseling and how they can be implemented. This chapter focuses on a general process to get a new research program ready for use in your field.

The General Process

1. An issue has to be identified.

An issue will arise that needs to be resolved. This could include content that might be challenging or new. The person who organizes the study must find a reason why the issue has to be resolved.

2. A hypothesis for the project should be produced.

A hypothesis is a prediction that you feel will happen; it is an argument that you intend to prove. This should be stated so that the outcome is reasonable and be realistically predicted. You have to produce a hypothesis that can be measured.

3. The design of the project has to be made ready.

The project should be arranged based on what you want to look up and analyze. The design can work in many forms, although the content involved should be explored with care. You can work with as many people in the project as necessary, although a realistic total should be considered when you look for something that works for your studies.

You can design the project with a series of variables. The independent variable should be something that can be adjusted on your end. After that, a dependent variable must be established with the variable being the one that would be adjusted by the independent one. You can produce a graph or chart listing details on what the project entails; the independent layout would be on the X-axis. The dependent portion goes on the Y-axis.

Also, the variables should be ones that are easy to control and relevant to the task at hand. While the variables can be prepared in many ways, you will have to look well at how the variables are arranged and that you have an idea of what you will get here. The best thing to do for your needs is to produce content that is simple and does not entail anything frustrating. The variables must also be easy to measure throughout the entire process.

4. Decide how people are to participate.

The task will include people to participate and they should be carefully chosen. You might provide disclosure information about the task. Also, you have to decide how the participants are to participate.

5. The project can be carried out.

You could produce a process based on factors like how people are exposed to certain things or how people might change their behaviors when they know what is happening. Be prepared to look at many ways that the independent variable may be adjusted.

Sometimes the process will involve people not knowing what is happening. In other cases, those people might be told to fill out questionnaires or complete certain tasks. You could change some groups based on what you want to review. A control group with no variables may be used as a comparison. The groups should all be organized so you can identify how each one is operating.

6. The results should be collected.

You can look at the results based on how you are changing these variables and how people are responding to the test. You might also have to spend extra time to ensure you'll get enough people to respond to your research. It could take weeks or even months for you to determine what is happening with your group.

7. The results can be analyzed.

The analysis should include sensible charts and graphs that allow you to determine the content. You must also ensure the way you gather the data for your project is arranged so that the content is easy to follow and use.

8. A discussion should be made at the end.

A suitable discussion will provide you with an opportunity to analyze the results of the study and detail how the data you gathered is organized. The discussion should provide a sensible conclusion.

The key point is to ensure you know how the results relate to your hypothesis. There is always a chance that your hypothesis may be proven correct, but it could also be proven wrong.

Key Principles

The program that you wish to conduct needs to include a number of principles.

1. You must aim to produce results that are reliable. These include results that will help produce unique products or services.

2. There must be a sensible meaning based on the value of the subject matter and how well the content can work.

3. The method involved should be clear and sensible. Everything needs to be laid out so that other people could potentially reproduce the test themselves.

4. The knowledge being generated should be practical. There has to be a realistic consideration for why something is true.

5. There must also be a sense of meaning for the program. The research should include answers that are relevant to the needs of the person who is working on the task.

6. The ethical considerations surrounding the task must be addressed. This may include discussing the payments for participation or benefits that people might receive.

7. Collaboration is a must for research programs. Such projects can be extensive and complex and could be impossible to complete on one's own. You'll have to show that there's a smart approach to what is done.

8. The social context should be considered according to the complicated details and how extensive the work might be.

Having an organized project will ensure your task is easy to follow. It can be easy for you to learn more about your field or to help those who want to make a difference when the best research project is made ready.

Chapter 13 – Orientation and Ethics

The concerns surrounding ethics in the counseling process can be complicated. There are ethical standards that have been made clear for today's counselors. These have been produced by the American Counseling Association in the form of the ACA Code of Ethics. Produced in 2014, the code is thorough and has been made available on the ACA's website.

Six Key Principles

Ethics are based on many principles:

1. There must be a sense of autonomy supported by the counselor. The person who needs counseling must have the right to take full control of their life.

2. Nonmaleficence is critical for the success of a counselor. This is avoiding any actions that might potentially cause harm.

3. Beneficence means the work that is being conducted by the counselor is for the good of the people who need help the most.

4. Justice refers to having a sense of fairness and control over how the sessions are conducted.

5. Fidelity involves honoring all commitments or principles that are to be used in pursuing and developing sensible relationships that all people can agree upon.

6. Veracity is about being truthful and direct.

Ethics

Consider the points surrounding ethics as the ACA Code of Ethics states:

1. The client's welfare must be protected.

All records and documents regarding the client should be handled with care. This includes ensuring that the client's data kept private and confidential. The support group that a person wants to have on hand should be respected in the process. Your goal as a counselor is to ensure the client is kept positive and that there is a suitable plan to offer help to the client who needs services from you.

2. Informed consent in the treatment process.

You have to see that your client provides you with written consent for services. You must list information about the intent of the counseling sessions.

3. You must not impose values on other people or harm them in any way.

A counselor must ensure that a client is not to be harmed or abused in any way. This includes seeing that the client is treated with respect and care. You cannot inflict your values on other people if they disagree.

4. You cannot take part in any non-counseling roles.

Non-counseling roles include sexual or romantic relationships, which are prohibited. You should not provide counseling services to anyone with whom you have had romantic or sexual relations in the past. You cannot provide counseling services to family members.

5. Any changes to your professional relationship have to be addressed.

You need to let your clients know that you are making changes to your professional services. These include changes to your range of services or where you are based. You have to inform your clients about your intentions. You must ensure your clients have proper referrals so they can continue to get the help they need.

6. You must be respectful of the needs of the client even if you have to terminate a contract.

The contract that you have might have to be terminated. You can refer the client to another counselor. You must ensure the client's requirements are taken care of if you are not capable of providing the services that someone might require.

7. Respect is a necessity for the work you put in.

You have to show respect to your clients. This includes respect for privacy that a client has. You must also explain the limitations of what you are able to do.

8. There may be times you will be required to disclose information.

Sometimes you might have to break the confidentiality, such as in cases when someone has threatened self-harm or harming others. Details about communicable diseases may need reporting. You may also need to disclose information if a legal authority requires it or if the client says that they agree.

9. Records must be kept.

All records that you produce should be comprehensive and thorough while also being confidential unless something happens that requires you to share the data with others. You should also allow your clients to have full access to your records if needed. You should also allow other people related to the client to see the information only if the client says they agree to share the information.

10. Any relationships you have with other professionals should be with the respect of your clients in mind.

You cannot start relationships with other professionals if you are unable to keep the details surrounding your clients private and secure. You must ensure that other professionals do not have access to the records surrounding your clients unless those clients agree to use their services. You should not discuss information about your clients. If anyone that you might work with asks you about your clients, you should state that you are unable to disclose that information.

11. Any research projects that you plan must be done with the consent of your clients in mind if possible.

You should ensure that your clients will not be harmed during any research project you wish to plan. You must disclose information about what you are doing with those clients and ensure they recognize the reasoning for the task. Any discomforts or risks involved should be discussed in detail.

The extensive details of the ACA Code of Ethics can be found on the ACA's website.

Test #1

Human Growth and Development

1. The development of formal operations in Piaget's theory of cognitive development includes which of the following concepts?

   a. Abstract logic

   b. Space and quantity

   c. Object identification

   d. Concrete ideas

2. Kohlberg's theory of moral development during the conventional stage includes which of the following ideas?

   a. Avoiding punishment

   b. Establishing a sense of individualism

   c. The development of interpersonal relationships

   d. Social contracts

3. Erikson states that a person's development will include which of these concepts during the latest stage in one's life?

   a. Will

   b. Care

   c. Competence

   d. Purpose

4. Which of the following is not an example of extrinsic motivation?

    a. A student wants to complete a test to get a good grade.

    b. A person works harder to earn more money.

    c. A child wants to behave properly in the hopes of earning candy.

    d. A person takes vitamins to improve one's health.

5. A student who did not do well in their studies may say, "The textbook was too difficult" or "The ideas are frustrating." This is an example of:

    a. Self-serving bias

    b. Compensation

    c. Differentiation

    d. External factors

6. What develops with the classic aging pattern with regards to completing an intelligence test?

    a. Verbal scores increase

    b. Verbal scores decrease

    c. Nonverbal scores increase

    d. Nonverbal scores decrease

7. A person's behavior is explained as being something based on their specific situation. For instance, a man who works hard is described as being "professional" or "strong." This may be a sign of:

    a. Attribution

    b. Accusation

    c. Generalization

    d. Contradiction

8. A failure to allow the concept of age integration to move forward will result in:

    a. Stratification

    b. Reorganization

    c. Social lag

    d. Conformity

9. What existential question does Erikson argue may be posed during adolescence relating to one's general purpose in life?

    a. Who am I?

    b. Is it fine for me to be who I am?

    c. How can I love?

    d. What can do I to make my life count?

10. Which answer is best to describe why a person would become increasingly depressed as they reach old age?

    a. Lack of income

    b. General aging

    c. Career changes

    d. Location of residence

11. Occupational prestige may be identified based on which of the following?

    a. The unique nature of the job at hand

    b. The amount of work that is put into completing tasks in a field

    c. How much money the job pays

    d. The desirability of the job based on the role one has in society

12. A person who appears to have developed a stronger sense of socioeconomic status could have developed this point in one's life due to which of the following?

    a. A person began learning to read at a very early age.

    b. Joint attention was brought onto the person who needed support.

    c. Additional money was spent on one's education.

    d. All of the above.

Answers for Human Growth and Development

1. a. Abstract logic in the formal operations segment relates to reasoning and how well a person may develop certain ideas. Concepts that are learned in one context can be planned based on counterfactual ideas. This stage begins at around 11 years of age. Space and quantity are learned a few years earlier during the concrete operational stage of the theory. The ability to identify certain ideas or objects should be noted earlier on in one's life, although those abilities will become more prominent over time.

2. c. The concepts of avoiding punishment and producing individualism develop in the pre-convention stage during the early stages of one's life. The conventional stage involves the development of relationships and identifying the social roles one is to follow. The social contracts occur in the post-conventional stage during adulthood.

3. b. The will and purpose are identified before one's school age, particularly before the age of 5. Competence appears after the student enters school. Care occurs late in one's life, particularly in adulthood, as that person begins to understand how to care for other individuals and to respect the needs of others. At this point, a person should have already developed a purpose in life and should have the competence needed to move forward with what one wishes to do. The care stage is about resolving the concerns one has surrounding how well certain actions or functions develop in one's mind.

4. d. A person is working with the internal motivation for wanting a better life because that person is more likely to feel positive about the efforts they put into the work. Extrinsic motivation occurs when a person is working to achieve certain results based on external forces. While intrinsic motivation involves a person thinking about personal effects or better health, the other examples in this question describe people getting special rewards from outside. These include rewards like money or other special things that one might be entitled to as compensation for the work one does.

5. d. External factors are blamed when something does not work as well as one might have hoped. Blaming anything other than one's self is an attempt to prove they are smarter or more proficient than what they really might be. Self-serving bias is when a person focuses on internal actions when they are successful in their work.

6. d. Nonverbal scores tend to decrease according to the classic aging pattern. However, verbal results will be stable. The concern may be due to a person struggling to come up with deeper thoughts but still being able to resolve some of

the larger questions or concerns that they might have. Being able to express ideas nonverbally may be easier especially when a person struggles to find words.

7. a. The person in this example is interpreted as being hard-working. The arguments cannot be interpreted as accusations in that they are not trying to challenge something. They should not be seen as generalizations either, as the person could potentially engage in other behaviors at other times.

8. c. The age integration theory states that concepts of education, work, and leisure are expected to be consistent throughout one's entire life. This includes following several standards for education as new skills may expand one's knowledge and provide a person with a better idea of what one can do in the future. Social lag may inhibit a person from understanding what one can do. Conformity is adhering to what the majority is doing.

9. a. Adolescence is a time of self-discovery and exploration. In this case, a person in one's pre-teen and teenage years will start to discover the things that one is interested in. Answer B relates to preschool age and involves understanding the difference between right and wrong. Answers C and D relate to adulthood, and answer C is more for those in the early stages of adulthood and answer D relates to later years.

10. a. Although all of these factors can negatively influence a person, changes in one's livelihood and lack of income may be a greater influence leading to depression. As a person reaches the age of 65, they are more likely to develop depression due to factors like a decline in health, a lack of people in one's life, or a reduced ability to make in an income. There are situations where a person is not too concerned about income, but income will still be critical due to being able to afford health care and other basic needs.

11. d. Occupational prestige may be determined by whether a person finds rewards based on the tasks one completes. Prestige may also come from the benefits that one contributes to society or whether the job is respected. Sometimes occupational prestige may include salary earned for the job done, although this is not always the case. A person's ability to have a position where one can earn respect and trust from other people is a vital factor in receiving occupational prestige.

12. b. Joint attention refers to multiple individuals being focused on the development of something or some idea. From a developmental standpoint, this could be two people supporting the development of a child. The effort may involve the child being educated in a suitable environment or the child being taught well. The speed at which a child becomes literate or the amount of money that was spent on

helping a child to develop will not have as great an impact on growth as parents communicating well with the child.

Social and Cultural Diversity

1. A woman recently adopted a child from a former Soviet country. The woman is worried about what the child will need because the child comes from a different culture. What should you tell the woman?
    a. All children will make the same responses and actions regardless of the cultures they are part of.
    b. A professional should be consulted based on how one could communicate with a newborn.
    c. Participate in a parenting class to understanding how children behave and act
    d. Find literature about how different types of behaviors or activities may be considered to help children learn.

2. The Hawthorne effect suggests that:
    a. A person will engage in different behavior when there's a reward involved.
    b. A person's behavior will change when they know that they are being observed.
    c. The person feels removed from certain ideas when they are not related to anyone within a particular situation.
    d. There are no distinct changes when certain activities or behaviors are exhibited.

3. A manager at a workplace might tell a Muslim coworker not to lay out a prayer rug in their office and to use it to pray towards Mecca during the designated times of the day when this is necessary. The manager might argue that the Muslim worker's actions may cause others in the workplace to feel uncomfortable. The actions should be interpreted by a counselor as being:
    a. Unethical
    b. Egotistical
    c. Culturally sensitive
    d. Apathetic

4. Cross-cultural counseling is a practice that entails an understanding of how cultures may influence relationships. The attitudes and beliefs that a counselor should consider are:
    a. Recognizing image concerns surrounding other people
    b. The attitudes that people hold about other cultures
    c. Identifying indigenous concepts and attitudes
    d. All of the above

5. A counselor may potentially interpret behavior in some manner regardless of the cultural context. That counselor is operating with a:
    a. Blind review
    b. Unbiased report
    c. Cultural bias
    d. Quick judgment

6. Many minorities in the United States are less likely to seek mental help than their counterparts who follow different religions. Why are minorities not as likely to do this?
    a. There is not enough money to afford insurance for services.
    b. Stigmas surrounding the treatment process
    c. A lack of access to treatments
    d. All of the above

7. A counselor should talk with a person about the processes involved with a psychological analysis of intervention. The counselor should discuss which of the following:
    a. A person's legal rights
    b. Medications for use
    c. Alternative therapy solutions
    d. Ideas for managing one's work

8. A white counselor is working with a black client. The counselor is asked by the client whether or not the counselor will treat him/her differently due to race. The counselor will state that race is not going to be a factor. How can this be interpreted?
    a. Objectivity
    b. Transference
    c. Micro-invalidation
    d. Attitude adjustment

9. Cultural insensitivity can be interpreted as:
    a. Assuming a person is of one particular culture without considering other ideas
    b. Assuming that all people within one culture are the same
    c. Not recognizing the values that a person has in their culture
    d. All of the above

10. What is macroculture?
   a. The dominant culture in a group
   b. The only culture you'll find in a group
   c. The tenants dictating how cultures in one group are formed
   d. A culture that can only expand to a specific size

11. Propinquity may influence how well some people may behave during particular activities. What does propinquity refer to?
   a. People who have the same beliefs
   b. Those who are confident
   c. People of the same race
   d. People living near one another

Answers to Social and Cultural Diversity

1. a. The general responses that children and adults have may be interpreted as universal. This includes vocal or physical responses. The words that are utilized may be different, although the general actions should be consistent.

2. b. The Hawthorne effect, which is also called the observer effect, occurs when a person knows that they are being noticed. The effect may be observed in cases where the lighting in a work area or study area is enhanced or more security cameras are positioned in the space. The people involved will attempt to act differently or show a sense of responsibility when they know they are being observed.

3. a. The action is unethical as it keeps a person from having the right to express their faith. Counselors must ensure that people do not discriminate against people based on their faith.

4. c. Indigenous attitudes should be considered based on what people of various cultures might have expressed or felt over time. These attitudes may illustrate certain ideas or attitudes they have.

5. c. A cultural bias may develop when a person attempts to make a generalization. This includes assuming that one person may engage in a particular behavior or action based on the culture they are a part of. A counselor will need to research the cultures they are encountering to eliminate the risk of cultural bias.

6. b. Although A and C could potentially be correct, B is the most likely answer. There may be cultural stigmas in certain demographics, particularly in the African and Asian communities, suggesting that people who try to seek help for their mental concerns may be judged unfairly. Other sensible factors involved include income inequalities or minorities living in parts of the country where it may be difficult to find a counselor.

7. a. The legal rights that a person has regarding one's mental health needs may be discussed. A counselor may also talk about things like the goals and expectations that the client has. The rights should also be discussed during the orientation process so as the client will understand and recognize the concepts being supported by the sessions. Talking about medications may not be appropriate as medications often are inadequate or frequently produce certain risks, thus keeping B from being an appropriate answer.

8. c. Objectivity would not work here, as that requires having a specific goal. Micro-invalidation is critical as it reduces the feelings and thoughts surrounding race. Whether or not micro-invalidation works will depend on the client. While someone might say that he or she "does not see color," the other person might feel as though this is not true.

9. d. Each of these answers can be interpreted as part of cultural insensitivity. For instance, a person might assume that a black person has ancestry from Africa. But that black person might actually have Central American, the United Kingdom, or Australian ancestry. There might be cases where a person assumes that a black person should be interested in the same things that some other black people. Each of the answers suggests generalizations and stereotyping.

10. a. In most cases, you will come across multiple cultures. These cultures can include various aspects or differences that make them unique, but the most important point about these cultures is that they are varied in size. Macroculture is the most dominant culture in an area.

11. d. Propinquity is how well people behave based on how well they can link with one another. In this case, people might be more attracted to one another when they are physically close to each other. This is regardless of any other demographics or beliefs that they might have as individuals. For instance, people who are in the same apartment complex might be more attracted to each other due to being in close proximity with one another all the time.

Helping Relationships

1. What makes transference and counter-transference different in a review?

    a. How the blame for a situation is shared between parties

    b. Who is in charge of the conversation between the counselor and the patient

    c. How much of an effort is needed in to consult two people

    d. How a relationship is transferred between parties

2. Self-disclosure may be encouraged by the counselor during a consultation. When would it be appropriate for a person to engage in self-disclosure?

    a. To control or manipulate the thoughts that the patient has

    b. When trying to ask questions of the participant

    c. To introduce oneself

    d. To enhance the collaborative nature of the consultation sessions

3. Adler states that a person will develop their personality traits through external factors. This is a critical aspect of his theory of individual psychology. Which of the following could be interpreted as an external factor in Adler's view regarding the development of relationships between different parties?

    a. Compensation

    b. Sacrifice

    c. General self-worth

    d. Attitudes towards concepts

4. Spitting in the client's soup is the name of a type of intervention that may be used in the individual psychology process. What is this process?

    a. Avoiding traps that people often fall into

    b. Identifying the motivations behind certain behaviors that people might engage in

    c. Making certain motivations that one has unappealing and undesired

    d. Explaining the negativity of the situation

5. According to Karen Horney, the potential for people to grow their relationships and to be more positive starts at this point in life:

    a. Birth

    b. Adolescence

    c. Early adulthood

    d. Late adulthood

6. A patient is telling you about how he has been trying to stop gambling recently. However, he also mentioned that recently he picked up a lottery ticket at his local convenience store. He states that he did not think about what he was doing and that he did not recognize the issue until well after he bought his ticket. What part of the person's mind caused this to develop:

    a. Subconscious mind

    b. Id

    c. Ego

    d. Superego

7. A patient is talking about how she was in an abusive relationship but is trying to get away from the topic. She says that she does not want to think about what had happened to her in the past. The issue here is an example of:

    a. Repression

    b. Suppression

    c. Displacement

    d. Reactionary attitude

8. A person who engages in identification will do so by taking the qualities of someone else or another role. This may be a person not identifying one's name, but rather the position that someone might have in the workplace or the duties that the person has. Why would someone participate in this way of identification?

    a. To reduce anxiety

    b. To enhance one's image

    c. To make people feel that someone is serious or dedicated to something

    d. To rationalize whatever is being done at a time

9. Adlerian therapy allows you to engage at the beginning of a healthy relationship with a client. What should be included at the beginning of your conversation with the client to determine what he/she needs?

    a. Identify the astrological sign of that person.

    b. Review the general reasons why they are seeking help for ongoing issues.

    c. Determine the prior psychological history

    d. Assess the personal history of the client based on birth order and early memories

10. A person-centered approach to helping someone with relationships could be used when looking at certain behaviors while also supporting the ongoing concerns of the client. What quality must a counselor express when working with a client during a person-centered approach?

    a. Congruency

    b. Positive thoughts

    c. Empathy

    d. All of the above

11. How can you tell that you are experiencing transference when working with a client?

    a. You don't feel as much control over what is happening in a situation as what you have been used to experiencing.

    b. You start to think differently about what you're managing.

    c. You start to tire of whatever your client is saying or doing.

    d. You are starting to experience feelings that are beyond what you are normally used to.

12. Rationalization often helps to make something sound sensible during an argument. Part of this is to convince people that some attitude or action is worthwhile. Why do people engage in rationalization?

    a. To avoid judgment

    b. To defend their attitudes

    c. To project feelings towards others

    d. To change the subject in a discussion

13. The ego can be used to defend a relationship or a feeling. Much of this may be done in order:

    a. To prevent anxiety

    b. To keep someone from being taken advantage of by another party

    c. To cause a person to feel positive about one's life

    d. All of the above

14. Multiple dates are to be determined when using Bowen's family theory to identify considerations of the particular events that are influencing family members. What types of dates should be collected?

    a. When certain job changes took place

    b. Vacations that one participated in

    c. General routines that one participates in throughout the day

    d. Personal physical concerns

15. A person who is a middle child may express the following:

    a. The characteristics of a younger sibling

    b. The characteristics of an older sibling

    c. Both A and B

    d. None of the above

16. Emotional cutoff may develop in some relationships. The concept occurs due to:

    a. A person trying to hide certain feelings or attitudes at a time

    b. Issues where someone might be unhappy with one's personal attitudes

    c. A person being upset over certain things developing at one's current stage in life

    d. A person having unresolved emotional issues with one's parents

17. The multigenerational transmission process is a concern that might influence how certain feelings are conveyed during a relationship with other people. The transmission should be explored cautiously based on the things that have changed over time between multiple people. The process can be noticed based on:

    a. Certain changes that might develop based on attitudes

    b. How far removed a person is from certain generations that might have developed differently

    c. The stability of one's life based on certain attitudes or thoughts

    d. None of the above

18. What should not be done if you plan to offer a Rogerian attitude to identify concerns with a client?

    a. Diagnose a client

    b. Ask why something is important to a client

    c. Deciding what should and should not be brought up at any time

    d. Determining past events that could have influenced a certain feeling

19. Gestalt therapy may be used to resolve certain issues that people have in relationships. The practice would include which of the following to identify concerns among clients:

    a. Delving into past events

    b. Reviewing questionnaires

    c. Role-playing

    d. Discussing the evolution of a relationship

20. Arnold Beisser argues that the paradoxical theory of change may be used as part of Gestalt therapy. The paradox, in this case, states that a person may attempt to be someone that they are not. The end result would be:

    a. The person behaves the opposite of how they have been behaving.

    b. That person will continue to have the same attitudes.

    c. Trying to act like a different person from a prior relationship.

    d. A person becoming too confrontational .

21. What type of error may develop when trying to review the assumptions that can happen in a study of what someone is trying to do?

    a. A person will act the same way in real life as they do in a counseling session.

    b. A person could act like they did years ago.

    c. Someone is not going to be less supportive of others.

    d. A relationship may improve if the status quo remains and the people involved try to work to resolve the situation.

22. Carl Whitaker's attitudes towards analyzing relationships between family members or romantic partners include the following concept:

    a. Experiential activities

    b. Structured thoughts

    c. Conscious thought

    d. Symbiotic feelings towards one another

23. The main goal of having people experience each other's behaviors or thoughts is:

   a. To try and ensure people don't spread too much information

   b. To allow for a relationship to remain intact and secure without the risk of further damage

   c. To decide on the right solution to resolve certain concerns

   d. Keep people from being defensive with one another

24. The object relations theory states that people are going to be attached to certain items more than others. Part of this includes looking at the general value of certain things that people might be interested in. What should be interpreted as the most important object relation that a person has?

   a. The relation with one's mother

   b. Any sleeping spaces that one had at an early age

   c. Any objects that one might have carried around when younger

   d. How well a person can link to another sibling

25. A libidinal ego may relate to a particular object based on:

   a. How often a person might try to get in touch with a certain aspect of life

   b. How exciting that object might be

   c. Whether the object in question is good or bad

   d. If the object is something suitable for one's life

26. What is the greatest concern surrounding the object relations theory?

   a. Too much emphasis on the mother

   b. People being considered active victims of parental problems

   c. Simplification of motives or feelings that people might have

   d. Concentrating too much on the positive aspects

27. Psychodynamic psychotherapy may help identify troubling points in relationships that may trigger depression and other negative symptoms. Part of this is the use of:

    a. Explaining the past

    b. Determining concerns that might have been triggered by medication use

    c. Reviewing why certain actions developed

    d. Free association

28. Dream interpretation may be used to identify certain feelings or thoughts that people have within their relationships. This is for cases where you are trying to identify concepts in a relationship relating to:

    a. What a person truly feels about their partner in the relationship

    b. How intense the worries or other concerns they have developed might be

    c. How much value a person puts into the intensity of the relationship

    d. The general potential for the relationship to move forward or become stronger

29. Humanism is critical to the process of counseling based on the relationships they can develop. Part of this includes looking at the human aspects of someone who understands certain concepts. What could be interpreted as the basic view of people through humanism?

    a. A person's parents will play the greatest role in shaping how someone might develop.

    b. A person is capable of making their own decisions.

    c. People are often difficult to understand; they may become angry rather quickly.

    d. People have strong drives.

30. A person-centered approach to understanding the needs and concerns should be managed with the following in mind:

    a. Identifying the personal attitudes that one holds

    b. Recognizing the influences of one's life

    c. Recognizing future potential

    d. All of the above

31. The existential theory is identifying concerns in relationships based on:

    a. Finding ways to control the effects of depression

    b. Recognizing the ways a person might try to defend certain situations that have developed in one's life

    c. The value or purpose of one's life

    d. Understanding the possible changes that may occur in one's life

32. The physical dimension may be utilized in the existential theory of relationships to identify how people may feel about their health, how much money they have, and how close they are to other people. However, the physical dimension may not necessarily be a way to analyze people in every situation. What is the main problem surrounding being overly dependent on the physical dimension of this theory?

    a. The emotional attitudes are more important than what is physically in one's world.

    b. A person might have different attitudes of what is and is not good for the body.

    c. There might be concerns about how different ideas can develop.

    d. Some of the physical benefits of life are only temporary.

33. If you were to try to have people focus on certain concepts in their relationships, you would focus on which of the following strategies?

    a. Visualization

    b. Reflection

    c. Role-playing

    d. Dream interpretation

34. What may be enhanced in one's life when Gestalt therapy is used?

    a. Awareness

    b. Self-esteem

    c. Clarity

    d. All of the above

35. Narrative therapy is a part of managing relationships that often includes:

    a. People determining their situations by looking at their ongoing stories

    b. Determining what people might feel about themselves

    c. Identifying concerns based on emotions

    d. Deciding what might happen in the future

36. Two people in a relationship are communicating with each other through different ego states. The two communications can result in a negative reaction with one another. The transaction in question can be interpreted as a:

    a. Crossed transaction

    b. Ulterior transaction

    c. Antagonistic transaction

    d. Complementary transaction

Answers to Helping Relationships

1. d. The relationship between the two parties is the main point to analyze in this situation. In transference, the emotions that a person has in a relationship are conveyed to the therapist. In countertransference, the therapist is the one who will convey the feelings for the patient and attempt to influence the discourse. The therapist may recognize attitudes of what someone is thinking, but it can go in the other direction if the therapist is aiming to influence the attitudes of the client.

2. d. Self-disclosure helps people in a situation to feel more comfortable with one another. This happens by way of feedback and the people involved have a better idea of what to expect from one another.

3. a. Compensation is a part of individual psychology that may be used in a study. The idea of compensation is that a person would try to alter their behaviors in order to compensate or make up for any problems they have. They attempt to enhance their image or value, although this may also result in that person engaging in over-compensation.

4. b. Spitting in the client's soup is a practice that involves determining why someone might engage in certain behaviors. The goal is to keep that person from continuing those attitudes or actions. A is another part of individual psychology known as avoiding the tar baby. C and D are the alternative solutions of pushing the envelope where a person learns that certain things one is doing may not be advisable.

5. a. People may develop stronger relationships at birth. According to Horney, a person has the ability to handle certain attitudes surrounding development throughout life without any inhibitions.

6. b. The id, according to Freud, is the part of the mind responsible for impulses. The ego would normally be responsible for the person to avoid a situation by trying to explain the realism involved. The client's id may have interfered and caused them to gamble even if they were trying hard to avoid gambling.

7. b. Suppression is a person actively attempting to block memories and situations from the past in order to forget them. This is the opposite of repression, an action where a person's memories are unconsciously forgotten after some time, thus resulting in memory loss of the event.

8. a. Although identification is often used to make a person look more attractive and striking to the public, the main reason for identification is to keep a person from

feeling anxious about what they are doing. This includes ensuring fears can be reduced and kept under control.

9. d. The Adlerian therapy process requires you to assess a client's history after you start a healthy and positive relationship with them. You should ask about their birth order in the family and prior memories to determine what might have influenced their development in the past. The practice causes the Adlerian therapist to be an ideal person to hire to obtain information on students and how their behaviors might impact their lives.

10. d. A counselor has to be congruent or in agreement with someone about the attitudes or thoughts that one wishes to convey. Meanwhile, the counselor may also show positive regard for the things that one says or feels like a means of showing understanding and producing feelings of rapport. The positive regard must be unconditional at all times. Empathy must also be expressed to show the client that their feelings or thoughts are understandable and are recognized.

11. d. Transference develops in a relationship when the client starts to influence the feelings that the counselor might have. This could directly change certain things or may help get both sides of the relationship to work on the same page.

12. b. Rationalization works to make certain ideas more interesting and to keep concepts from being repeated.

13. a. The ego can create a sense of rationality and understanding surrounding what one wishes to think about. This includes looking at possible changes that might take place based on what someone might be thinking. However, the ego may cause someone to think irrationally unknowingly. Part of this comes from the ego changing one's reality and making it harder for thoughts to develop accordingly.

14. a. The family theory states that dramatic events that directly influence one's relationships, ability to earn money, or ability to provide things for the family may have a greater influence on relationships than other factors. Dates of job changes and the dates of major family crises or any significant life events that took place like weddings, divorces, or funerals should be noted. The key is to identify how these events might influence a relationship and if any significant changes took place as a result.

15. c. The characteristics of the older and younger siblings can transfer to the middle child. The characteristics may be varied based on what might happen, although the specifics that would develop will vary based on the situations.

16. d. Emotional cutoff occurs in a relationship when someone has some issues with parents or other close family members. In some cases, a person might try to

curtail their ability to communicate with others due to those issues. The emotions can keep a person from forming appropriate relationships.

17. a. The attitudes that people might have held over time can change based on certain ideas that are delivered or the thoughts involved. One generation of a family might have felt a specific way about a topic, but another generation may act differently. Further questioning or analysis should be conducted to determine what people might be thinking while engaging in a relationship.

18. a. The Rogerian approach states that you should not try to diagnose a person with a certain condition. Diagnoses in the Rogerian study are not going to help people as this might produce certain attitudes that could cause harm. The process could cause a counselor to express judgment rather than try to delve deeper into certain feelings that a person might have.

19. c. The empty chair technique is frequently used in Gestalt therapy to identify the concerns that a client may have. The technique identifies concerns surrounding what people might be thinking or what could have caused another in a relationship to act in one way or another.

20. b. The paradoxical theory of change states that a person will continue to remain the same when trying to be like someone else. In some cases, that person will be even more the same as something in the past. A person might not be willing to accept what they have been doing. They are not trying to be unique, but rather want to change certain attitudes or feelings that they have.

21. a. There are often times that a person might try to behave differently. persona client may try to change their image in the counseling process. The sudden attitude changes might make it easier for someone to feel comfortable about what is happening while trying to keep the issues in a meeting from possibly being unacceptable.

22. a. The experiences that people have together are going to make a greater impact on the relationship than other factors. A 'here and now' concept may be used to determine what people feel now. The relationship between the client or clients and the counselor may be more important than any other ideas or attitudes.

23. d. Although the experiential knowledge that may be produced can prove to be less significant, you should look mainly at how people express their thoughts. You should attempt to keep people from trying to defend their actions and are unable to convey their feelings or attitudes with one another.

24. a. Since the mother is usually the first person a child will be attached to, it would not be surprising that this is the first relationship. D may be used in some cases, although this would be mainly for cases of multiple births.

25. b. The whole ego will focus something that might be intriguing and useful for one's life. The anti-libidinal ego will focus mainly on how a person relates to a bad or difficult object or situation. The libidinal ego will concentrate on things that might be interesting or exciting. In this situation, a person will react to the intriguing things that might change their attitudes and make it easier for them to think about the positive things that could happen. However, the whole ego may ignore some of the possible consequences that could develop.

26. a. A is correct because the mother is the main focal point of attention in a person's development. As important as the mother is, the father is not treated with as much importance. B is not correct because the theory could refer to people as passive victims of problems that were produced by the parents. C is also not correct because the theory has long been criticized for how there is no focus on clarity when it comes to how definitions are to be produced.

27. d. Free association may help identify personal conflicts. The process involves a free review of the things that one might have been thinking about in the past. The key is for the client to speak for him/herself, as Freud once described. The ideas of the analyst should not be repeated. Rather, certain words should be reviewed based on what one wants to do with certain concepts or attitudes that can develop. The goals of the treatment may also be very clear at this juncture.

28. a. Dream interpretation may require extensive analysis into understanding the concepts or values that have come about. This includes considering how a person thinks about someone and if the attitudes being conveyed are sensible or if changes should be made.

29. b. Humanism suggests that a person has the ability to exercise control over the things happening in their life. This includes working to resolve difficulties and to control the issues that they have in life. A person may also feel more positive about the things that occur when trying to change their life around.

30. a. A person's general attitudes may directly influence some of the things that one might be thinking about and how those attitudes may change over time. Determining and understanding these attitudes are critical.

31. c. The existential theory is recognizing the meanings that people have for things in their lives. People may use this to understand what they should be doing when attempting to help other people or make positive changes in the lives of people

who are close to them. The theory helps people to produce a healthy sense of change, although this is not necessarily the goal that people have to follow every time.

32. d. A person may become disillusioned with some of the physical things that come about in their relationships. This includes concerns relating to intimacy or sexuality as well as financial stability. A person could also realize after a while that the positive things that have come about in one's life are only temporary and that changes have to be made to keep their life from falling apart.

33. a. Visualization helps to recognize how certain ideas can develop and how those ideas can change behavior. A person may focus on the ways ideas are conveyed and how powerful those concepts might be.

34. d. Gestalt therapy explains how a person grows and can become a more positive person who has an understanding of what works and what is appropriate in one's life. All of the answers may be correct because they include helping a person to live a whole and positive life where one fully understands the things that need to be done in living a productive and happy life.

35. a. Narrative therapy requires a person to look at the things that have been happening in their life. The therapy can involve talking about someone's life and general actions.

36. a. A cross transaction occurs when the two people address ego states that are different from the ones that they are really in, thus resulting in difficulties in communication. The two sides are not being antagonistic, or at least not on purpose. This is different from an ulterior transaction where the ego states of the two people are different, but they are producing responses that come from the same ego state. A complementary transaction would occur when the two people involved have the same ego state.

Group Work

1. A norm may be established when looking at how people in a group behave. What is the norm supposed to be for keeping the group behaving appropriately?
    a. A surprising behavior that someone participates in
    b. Expected behaviors
    c. The behavior of the group in general and every person in the group
    d. The person who might put in the most effort

2. Yalom's interpersonal factors refer to ideas that should be shared by many people in the same group. Which of the following relates to helping other people in the same group?
    a. Altruism
    b. Guidance
    c. Instillation
    d. Imparting

3. Yalom cites that people are going to have to accept responsibility for some of the decisions that they make in their life. The idea of accepting responsibility refers to:
    a. Catharsis
    b. Universality
    c. Self-understanding behavior
    d. Existential behavior

4. Normative social influence is a concept where people try to conform to the pressures of other members of the group. Why would a person decide to conform?
    a. To facilitate a task
    b. To keep other people from becoming angry
    c. To be accepted
    d. To reduce the costs associated with keeping a group functional

5. There are four zones of interpersonal space that may be noticed between members of a group. Which zone is the furthest away from a person?

    a. Personal

    b. Social

    c. Selective

    d. Intimate

6. Informational social influence is a concept that states:

    a. The group knows more about something that a single person would

    b. The group has more qualities involved based on the skills people have

    c. A group can be as small or as large as it has to be

    d. Individuals can take charge at varying times when trying to produce something valuable

7. For the best results, how many people are ideal in a group?

    a. 4

    b. 6

    c. 8

    d. 10

8. What should be done within a group before the people involved can produce the norms needed to keep the group functional?

    a. The group must decide who is going to have the most power and control over the group

    b. People will initially determine how well the group will function and the goals of the group

    c. The initial formation can take place with nothing else happening

    d. People will consider some of the standards to follow in order to keep the norms intact or to determine what the norms will be

9. Many people in the same group are talking all at once. One member will say that the people need to stop talking for a moment and then plan a schedule to communicate with one another. The person who is asking for this is what type of character in this situation?
    a. Recorder
    b. Gatekeeper
    c. Facilitator
    d. Organizer

10. A dominator in a group session is someone who:
    a. Determines the path that the group conversation will follow
    b. Will identify the tasks that have to be discussed in the group session
    c. Will block people from trying to talk
    d. Determine a sense of order when trying to make the group more organized

11. What is the greatest concern surrounding the scapegoat in a group?
    a. There is an extremely high likelihood that a scapegoat would be found in any group
    b. People might destroy relationships in a group by trying to pin all the blame of a situation on one person
    c. The scapegoat will keep the real issues from being explored
    d. All of the above

12. Which of these types of groups can potentially be the largest in size?
    a. Marathon
    b. Encounter
    c. Therapy
    d. T-group

13. George has been dealing with intense stresses throughout his life. These stresses are keeping him from having a healthy social life and may also be causing him to become easily frustrated. What type of group would be best for George to join?
    a. Support
    b. Remedial
    c. Preventative
    d. Developmental

14. A group of people who are cheering for the same sports team is wearing the same colors as the team on the field. What type of group are they?
    a. Reference group
    b. Attractiveness group
    c. Star quality group
    d. None of the above

15. What can be paired with conformity so that the group may be influenced by social factors?
    a. Responsibility
    b. Acceptance
    c. Approval
    d. Obedience

16. People in groups often engage in altruism to ensure that all in the group are happy and that potential problems are resolved quickly. What is a critical aspect of altruism that must be followed for this to work?
    a. The person involved must have full control over the group
    b. There must be a sense of selflessness in the activities of the group
    c. There should be as much time as possible to allow changes to happen
    d. All of the above

Answers to Group Work

1. b. A norm is the expected behavior of people in a group. The norm is decided by the group according to the culture of the people involved. The norms can also change during the lifespan of the group.

2. a. Altruism is a practice of helping people and supporting them. Guidance technically is supporting people, but this is more about being nurturing. Instillation is providing a feeling that a person can use to develop hope and the potential for one to recover from significant problems. The process of imparting involves teaching a person about what one can do to keep certain problems in one's life from being worse or more harmful.

3. d. Existential behavior is people accepting responsibility for their behaviors. Self-understanding looking into the motivational factors that might have triggered certain things to happen. Universality involves all the people in the same group recognizing that everyone in the group has different feelings or attitudes that might be difficult to predict. Catharsis is about the release of feelings that people have towards one another.

4. c. Normative social influence involves people conforming to group pressures. For instance, a person might engage in something unhealthy like smoking cigarettes or even assist in a criminal action. That person would be impacted by normative social influence even if they were not willing. The influence develops because that person is afraid of being shunned by others in the same group.

5. b. The most remote space is the public zone if people are at least twelve feet away. C is incorrect as selective space is not one of the four zones. Since the public zone is not included among the choices, the social zone would be the correct option. The social zone is about four to twelve feet away from a person and allows room for another person to join a group. The personal zone is from two to four feet away and could be a private conversation that is not expected to be heard by other people. The intimate zone is less than two feet and the people would expect privacy or intimacy. (Be advised that the specifics on what is an appropriate space may vary according to culture.)

6. a. Informational social influence is when many people can work together and share their ideas and thoughts with one another. This may include people who have the same skill sets or those who differ. People are working to complete the same tasks with the belief that everyone in the group has enough knowledge to complete a task.

7. b. Six people in a group make it is easier for people to share information. A group with only four people might have limited information to share. A group of eight people might become rather unwieldy. A group of ten people or more could become hard to manage due to the lack of ability for people to accommodate the needs of all within the group.

8. a. The process of getting a group to work will encompass five steps. First, the group will form and operate. Second, the group will determine how the power structure in the group should be arranged. The norms will be evident at this juncture. After this, the group will engage and determine how well the group operates. The group will decide if it is necessary to meet again and when.

9. b. The gatekeeper is the person who keeps order within the group. The gatekeeper will determine who is going to speak and in which order. The organization will arrange to get the people together, while the recorder will take notes about the things that people say during group time.

10. c. A dominator will make efforts to block other people in the group by interrupting others. A dominator might try to be too authoritative and in control of the discussion. A dominator does not try to dictate the flow of the conversation or determine the roles for people in the group. A gatekeeper keeps order.

11. d. A scapegoat is someone who may be blamed for the problems that have developed within the group. The scapegoat may also be someone who is angry for some reason. Continuing to act as if there is a scapegoat involved in a situation can be threatening to the quality of the group.

12. b. The encounter group can be any number of people, although it is more often closer to ten. The group may be open-ended, although it may also have a specific theme or reason to meet. A marathon group can be about 20 to 40 people and can involve a weekend outing where many people are together working towards an objective. A T-group is a smaller group, maybe 10 to 15 people and will involve a specialized standard to follow. The therapy group involves fewer than ten people. Such a group may also be highly formal in arrangement and have a structure for how the meeting will take place.

13. c. George would benefit the most from a preventative group so he can learn strategies to prevent certain problems from developing in his life. A remedial group would not work because he is not in any situations where something has to be fixed; stresses are to be prevented, not fixed. A support group wouldn't help

George either because he needs to devise an individualized strategy to manage his own concerns. George does not have any developmental concerns, so a developmental group would not work for him.

14. a. A reference group is one that another group wishes to emulate. In this case, many people might cheer for the same sports team and wear the same outfits and colors. The general fan worship suggests that the team is the reference group because of how that group is respected by others.

15. d. Obedience is critical for everyone in a group to conform to the specific rules that the group has established. Acceptance is a part of imitation. Responsibility means that individuals in a group accept certain roles to ensure the group is cohesive and effective. Approval focuses more on creating good relationships and ensuring one's image may be seen as positive without any judgment being imposed on the people involved.

16. b. Selflessness is the most important aspect of altruism. A person who engages in altruism will not be judgmental of others in the same group. They do not ask for anything in return, such as a special benefit or consideration. They operate only for the benefit of the group.

Career Development

1. Super's career development theory states that a person goes through five stages. In which stage is the need to try out certain ideas or values and to decide what skills one needs to develop?

   a. Growth

   b. Exploratory

   c. Establishment

   d. Maintenance

2. Jeff is interested in working with electronics in the future. He values practical activities and focuses on producing things with results that are immediately noticeable. Which of the six quadrants of the interest inventory would Jeff qualify to be part of?

   a. Conventional

   b. Enterprising

   c. Investigative

   d. Realistic

3. Sandra is interested in work that includes the social aspect of the interest inventory. Which of the following activities would Sandra give the greatest focus?

   a. Persuading people to follow a certain political issue

   b. Mentoring students who are in a certain class

   c. Producing art pieces in public settings

   d. Creating distinct machines that help people in various jobs

4. Roger prefers to produce unique forms of art on topics relating to what people are interested in today. He enjoys producing these works and selling them. Which letters in the Holland model of vocational interest would suit Roger's work the most?

    a. ESA

    b. CES

    c. ARE

    d. SAR

5. Bandura's social cognitive theory states that several things will influence a person's observational learning. These include concerns that might influence one's performance and career. Which of the following factors will influence one's work?

    a. Expectations for what one will do

    b. Social concerns

    c. Monetary gains

    d. How long it will take to complete a task

6. Bandura refers to the destiny idea as a critical aspect of self-efficacy. This means that a person who has a greater sense of self-efficacy will experience which of the following points?

    a. The person will feel that his or her destiny is out of their control and that anything could happen.

    b. The person will feel as though he or she is in control of one's life.

    c. The behavior that one wishes to engage in should be explored to determine what changes must be made.

    d. New efforts should be made to change one's attitude.

7. What will the Occupational Outlook Handbook not provide a person when investigating an interesting career?

    a. Places that a person can go to receive training

    b. A prediction of where the job will go in the future

    c. The salary that one might expect

    d. The training that a person needs to secure a position

8. Ginzburg's theory of career development argues that children will experience a great difference between what they expect in a job and what the job entails in reality. When would the career goals that someone has become realistic in accordance with his particular theory of career development?

    a. 11 years of age

    b. 15 years of age

    c. 17 years of age

    d. 20 years of age

9. The concept of curiosity in Ginzburg's theory of career development is applicable only when:

    a. A child is pretending to be in a position.

    b. There are no changes involved with what one wishes to do in life.

    c. There are no resources involved with allowing something to work.

    d. A child is not aware of the general points of a certain profession.

10. The Myers-Briggs Type Indicator or MBTI has sixteen segments surrounding one's behaviors. What can be said about the healer segment of the MBTI?

    a. The task is more personal, although there is a sense of logic involved.

    b. Ideas are the main focus for people to review.

    c. There is a strict sense of technicality in the work.

    d. People are going to be in charge of others.

11. The MBTI states that decisions may be made between thinking and feeling functions. What can be noticed within the feeling segment?

    a. Logicality is critical when considering feelings.

    b. A person has to be tough when dealing with feelings.

    c. Questions can be proposed to decide solutions.

    d. There is an open-ended nature for events.

12. Mary is highly extroverted and does what she can to help other people and work with them. She works hard to think about ideas and use her intuition. But she is also highly perceptive and focuses on what can be done in a situation without being judgmental of others. For what type of position would Mary suit if the MBTI is considered?

    a. Field Marshall

    b. Inventor

    c. Promoter

    d. Supervisor

13. The choice stage of deciding on a profession should be planned at the beginning start of one's work. The choice stage depends on:

    a. The crystallization of a thought

    b. The clarification of a thought

    c. Going through the general exploration

    d. All of the above

14. According to Tiedeman, what is the most noteworthy aspect of the integration stage of moving into a job ?

    a. A person will go forward with implementing the choice.

    b. Changes start to take place within the work environment that the participant enters.

    c. The person will be accepted by the other group members through the general reception efforts.

    d. The newness involved with a position starts to wear off.

15. Which of the following is not one of the six occupations that Holland has incorporated in his work on the personality types that people hold and the jobs that they might enter?

    a. Enterprising

    b. Inventive

    c. Realistic

    d. Social

16. Joseph wishes to take in a position in the enterprising field based on Holland's occupations. What should Joseph ask himself when deciding whether or not this is appropriate for him?

    a. How much effort am I willing to put into analyzing and evaluating the ideas?

    b. How innovative am I in coming up with ideas for where I want to go with my work?

    c. How well can I organize the things I wish to do in my work?

    d. How well am I capable of working with data?

17. Anne Roe's personality development theory states which of the following skills would be required when trying to enter a communication job:

    a. An ability to handle written data

    b. Knowing how to design ideas

    c. Being sociable with other people

    d. Having an idea of how finances are to be managed

18. What is the most significant aspect of Anne Roe's personality development theory?

    a. The child has the right to determine their own identity.

    b. The child may attempt to rebel against their parents.

    c. A person has the right to try different jobs as soon as possible in their life.

    d. The parenting style that parents or guardians use will determine what role a child will play.

19. Anne Roe worked with Maslow's hierarchy of needs regarding the personality theory of choosing a career. Roe states that a child might have unmet needs surrounding their decisions. Which one of the following is expected to happen as a result of these unmet needs?

   a. There will be a sense of investment to educate oneself to keep on one's path.

   b. The person will change their career path based on trying to fill in the gaps in their life.

   c. The issues may be forgotten over time as the child starts to gravitate towards one particular position based on their patterns of behavior.

   d. No real changes are expected to occur.

20. If someone wants to have an enterprising career, their main goal should be to:

   a. Lead other people

   b. Produce as many sales as possible

   c. Consider a larger market share

   d. A and B

Answers to Career Development

1. b. The exploratory stage occurs from the ages of 15 to 24 according to Super's theory. A person will try out various activities and various work experiences and hobbies. The person also collects important information about possible jobs. The growth stage occurs earlier where the person is developing the capacity of understanding. The establishment stage is when the person is building skills and stabilizing their abilities through regular experience in the field of work. The maintenance stage appears later and involves continuous changes during the time of employment.

2. d. The realistic segment of the interest inventory is hands-on and practical functions. Jeff, in this example, would be interested in reality to produce tangible results in his work in electronics while building or fixing electronic items. The conventional segment refers to organizational efforts while focusing on efficiency; this includes a review of finances and specific forms of data. Enterprising focuses on selling things and being more assertive with people who might be interested in what is being offered. The investigative segment focuses on solving abstract problems that require concentration on intellect.

3. b. The social aspect of the interest inventory involves helping people and giving them advice. Teachers, counselors, and people who lead group discussions will fit with the social segment. A) focuses on the enterprising segment, while C) is about the artistic section. D) relates to the realistic section of the interest inventory.

4. a. The ESA letters refer to enterprising, social, and artistic endeavors. Roger delves into all three of these aspects as he focuses on producing unique works of art while concentrating on social considerations. The enterprising aspect refers to the work he puts into his efforts. The C and R letters are for conventional and realistic activities and would not qualify for what Roger does. I is for investigative and rounds out the six segments; this point would not apply in what Roger does for a living.

5. a. The expectations in one's activities relate to the outcome and solving problems. Other factors that can influence the learning process are the goals one has, values of the work, one's developmental status, and the general prestige that comes with the model that one wishes to plan and work with.

6. b. Self-efficacy is having a sense of control over one's destiny. That person can engage in many activities in life with the belief that completing the tasks and making efforts will allow someone to become more in control.

7. a. The Occupational Outlook Handbook or OOH is designed to help people understand the specifics of various jobs. The book is not designed to give people tips on what they can do to find jobs or to find information on where they can go to get training. What people can expect in certain jobs may be in the guide.

8. c. The first stage of the theory is the fantasy stage that includes the period from toddler to 11 years of age. The tentative state is the adolescent period from ages 11 to 17 when a person is considering possible career opportunities. The realistic stage starts at 17 and continues one's twenties. The student at this stage should have an idea of what they want to do and move into college or a trade school, hopefully, to study subjects in the area they are most interested in.

9. d. Curiosity is being interested in learning about something. The activities at an early age would involve the child beginning to learn about interests. At this point, the child is generally free to explore his interests.

10. a. The healer segment or the INFP segment refers to introversion, intuition, feeling, and perception. The healer is using personal actions to help people who may be experiencing negative situations. Counselors or psychologists are often healers. However, a sense of logic must also be used.

11. d. The MBTI part that deals with feelings discussed having an open-ended attitude to manage one's feelings. This is a casual approach that is tender and appreciative. A thinking process involves making decisions that are reasonable and closed-ended as well as critical.

12. b. Mary would fit in with the inventor position as she is extraverted, intuitive, focus on thinking, and does not judge them. A Field Marshall is someone who is judgmental of others. The promoter and supervisor positions are also focused on extraverted behaviors . All four of these positions focus on the logical aspects involved with completing tasks.

13. a. The answer is based on the Tiedeman and O'Hara analysis of how career choices may be made and what people can expect out of their employment. The choice occurs after the crystallization process. The exploration stage is the first of the stages and the choice stage is the third. The crystallization stage will focus on stabilizing the thoughts that one has. These ideas are the basis of the choices one will make. The clarification stage would occur well after the original choice is made. At this point, the choice may be reassessed to determine if it was the correct one.

14. d. D is the correct answer as it is the integration stage. During this stage, the newness of a job will start to wear off. The enthusiasm for a new job might start to diminish.

15. b. The inventive career path is not something that Holland considered when reviewing job paths. Rather, Holland has focused on the investigative path. The other answers are among the other paths that Holland developed.

16. c. The enterprising field concentrates on influencing people, persuading them to do things, and with organizing ideas. Organizational efforts will especially do well with economic ideas. A is more about the investigative field as it requires looking at the things one wishes to do with work and how ideas may be implemented. B is the artistic approach that focuses on creating things and designing possible innovations. Answer D is managing clerical and numerical data and with following general instructions and set procedures.

17. a. The communication aspects of the personality development theory depend on written and oral ideas to be conveyed and planned. B is about the arts, designing and creating unique things. C is the service setup and focuses on the social needs of talking with people and giving instructions. D pertains to the business segment and involves the management and finance aspects of work.

18. d. Roe argues that a person's career will develop due to factors that are inherent in birth, including genetic factors and the overall experiences that a child has. The general parenting style that a child is subjected to will particularly make a difference in how the child develops.

19. b. The person who has unmet needs might have a desire to resolve those needs before trying to go any further in his employment. The unmet needs could be extensive and possibly difficult, although these needs have to be resolved if a person wants to move forward with their studies.

20. a. Leading other people is the most important aspect of being in an enterprising position. The market share and sales can be useful, but they will not be worthwhile unless the enterprising position either has control over more things or has an ability to keep profits under control. A sales representative may be a good example of someone who is looking to lead people.

Assessment

1. A counselor may recognize a person is going through a crisis. What is the correct definition of a crisis?

    a. A person becoming weak

    b. A natural part of the development of the human mind

    c. A case where someone is going through problems that might be traumatic

    d. A state of mind

2. A child often requires extensive testing and assessment following a crisis. The child may require more than what an adult might need. Why would the child require more analysis?

    a. A child's reactions may be different from what an adult may experience.

    b. A child does not have the experience needed to handle a crisis.

    c. It may be difficult for a child to decide who to trust during or after a crisis.

    d. There might be a sense of irregularity involved in finding a solution.

3. Beck's depression inventory has 21 questions that a patient may answer. These multiple-choice questions are analyzed and graded to determine the level of depression that one has. The 21 questions are organized based on the general P values, or points where one aspect will be worth more on the test than others. Which of these points would have a larger P-value when compared with other questions?

    a. Feeling like a failure

    b. Sexual libido

    c. Fatigue

    d. Being overly critical of oneself

4. The Minnesota Multiphasic Personality Inventory or MMPI may help to identify certain personality traits in adults. The test is a review of many concerns in the client's life. Which of the following will not be analyzed in the MMPI?

    a. Work performance

    b. School issues

    c. Health status

    d. General obsessions

5. The Wechsler Adult Intelligence Scale is an intelligence quotient or IQ test that focuses on understanding verbal and performance-based functions. Part of this includes looking at the Working Memory Index or WMI. What is measured in the WMI as a part of the WAIS test?

    a. Arithmetic

    b. Vocabulary

    c. Searching for symbols

    d. Matrix reasoning

6. What is the greatest concern surrounding a self-report test?

    a. The ideas may be varied based on whoever is issuing the test.

    b. There are no standards as to where the test leads.

    c. The participant might be skewing the results.

    d. The details are not comprehensive.

7. A person answers certain tests on a test in some way but feels that the answers might not be correct or accurate. They only answered the questions in the belief that there's an acceptable way for how questions are to be answered. What is this phenomenon?

    a. Cultural test bias

    b. Interpretation bias

    c. Social desirability

    d. Personality factors

8. A multi-disciplinary team may be hired in a counseling firm to help you manage your patients. What would such a team do for you?

    a. Allow for various forms of discipline to develop due to certain actions

    b. Meet with individual people surrounding work

    c. Provide you with assistance in many fields

    d. All of the above

9. What concerns may be supported by a multi-disciplinary group with regards to assisting people?

    a. Traffic court issues

    b. Substance abuse

    c. School choice

    d. All of the above

10. Edward is struggling to stop smoking. He has been trying to control his desires for smoking, but he has not been able to work with cessation products or services. He feels that he might require counseling to help him deal with his addiction. Which of these therapy options would work best for him?

    a. Cognitive behavior therapy

    b. Adlerian therapy

    c. Person-centric therapy

    d. Gestalt therapy

11. Support groups are often organized to assist those who have gone through various traumatic events including a death in the family, an addiction, or a divorce. What may be noticed in a support group?

    a. People may allow their aggressive tendencies to be released.

    b. The participants will be capable of focus on other things in their lives.

    c. People work together in a safe environment.

    d. Medication use may be reviewed to identify what is working for the client.

12. Rational emotive behavior therapy may be used in the assessment process to identify what someone might be thinking. The therapy may work differently for cognitive therapy in many ways, including how REBT:

    a. Looks at the distortions that have developed in one's mind

    b. Is highly functional

    c. Looks at some of the cognitions that one has but does not involve anything too aggressive

    d. Provides a confrontational approach to the review process

13. Brief therapy includes twelve steps to identify some of the concerns that a person has and to also decide what might work to resolve certain problems that a person has. Which of the following twelve steps is the first one to appear among the four listed here?

    a. Connection

    b. Struggle

    c. Support

    d. Goals

14. Beck's Depression Inventory is designed to focus on:

    a. Determining how honest a person is regarding reporting their depression issues

    b. How significant a person's depression symptoms might be

    c. What medications a person requires to resolve depression

    d. Whether a person is experiencing a mood disorder

15. A solution-focused practice to resolve issues can identify some problems with something that is not working. What should be done if a solution is not working?

    a. Look at the source of why something wrong is happening

    b. Identify the person's aptitude to complete a task

    c. Try something different

    d. Wait for a moment

16. When employing a multi-modal therapy process, what is the main concern of an intervention?

     a. The intervention must include people who are as close to the subject matter as possible.

     b. The intervention needs to be completed early enough to keep a problem from becoming worse.

     c. The effort has to be explained to the participant well before the process itself can start.

     d. It is not easy to determine the concepts that someone might have.

17. You can use Lazarus' BASIC ID process to identify the personality that someone exhibits. In one situation, you might notice that a person is dealing with negative thoughts. What dimension of a person's personality may be noticed at this point?

     a. Affect

     b. Imagery

     c. Cognition

     d. Drugs

18. Music therapy can be used to help some people with many conditions and issues they have. Which of the following should you do when analyzing or assessing the things that someone is doing?

     a. Review the meanings for what someone is going through

     b. Understand how extensive or detailed the music might be

     c. Decide how long it takes to produce the music

     d. All of the above

19. An encounter group can be planned so you can identify how well people may interact with one another in the same group. This may include role-playing or other actions to help people learn more about each other and identify any mental concerns they may have. What should be done when planning an encounter group correctly?

    a. Review the tasks in which each member in a group will partake

    b. Determine what allows the members to interact with each other

    c. See what each person will do to support another

    d. All of the above

20. What is the most important consideration to review when working in a grief counseling session?

    a. The responses that a person has to a negative event.

    b. Any worries that someone has about how life might change.

    c. How well a person is able to adjust after a traumatic event.

    d. All of the above

Answers to Assessment

1. c. A crisis may be a single occasion, although it may be a recurring problem. Some crises may relate to natural disasters, family issues, or other concerns. A crisis is something that has become significant and may be difficult for a person to manage without help.

2. b. The experiences of a child are minimal in comparison with what an adult can handle. A is not the correct answer because the responses of a child to a crisis are often the same as an adult's responses. A child might become further isolated and uncomfortable because they do not have the language or understanding to make sense of the crisis. C is not the best answer because a child could trust various adults and should have an idea of who they can and cannot trust. It is up to a counselor to help resolve the worries that the child might develop following such a crisis.

3. a. Feeling as though one is a failure is a common sign of depression. This has one of the highest P values on the test. Other high-value factors are general feelings of sadness, a person feeling discouraged about one's future, disappointment in the self over past actions, a lack of interest in other people, and thoughts of suicide. B is incorrect because the sexual health of a person might not a concern, although it may become an issue. C is very low on the list and could be a sign of anything including some medical conditions. D is incorrect even though the P value of being overly critical is relatively high, that does not mean they might consider they are a failure.

4. a. Work performance does not appear anywhere in the MMPI. The test is about recognizing what causes people to act the way they do and not necessarily about end results. Some factors relating to one's job may link to the actual sections of the MMPI, including conduct problems or social discomfort. The other three choices refer to ongoing issues in one's life including cases where a person is not going to school when a person's health is in jeopardy and any particular obsessions that one is experiencing.

5. a. Arithmetic is a part of the WMI. This aspect of one's verbal IQ also entails understanding the sequencing between letters and numbers. The vocabulary part is found in the Verbal Comprehension Index, another part of the verbal IQ. A comprehension and information segment may be included as a part of the VCI within the test. The other two choices focus on a person's performance IQ. The symbols search is a part of the Processing Speed Index, and the matrix reasoning aspect is part of the Perceptual Organization Index and block design.

6. c. A self-report test is one where the participant will produce one's own report. The report is read by a reviewing party to discover what a person's emotional or mental concerns might be. The self-report test might allow the test-taker to feel comfortable, but there is a chance that the person might not always be honest. The participant might be too afraid to talk about certain things. As a result, the test might not be representative of their true behaviors.

7. c. Social desirability is a person trying to fit in with the rest of the crowd rather than trying to be unique. This is not a subjective issue because the person is not answering questions according to their personal beliefs. This is not a part of cultural bias because a person's culture is not being considered.

8. c. The multi-disciplinary approach involves many people in various fields of work coming together to help identify the needs that the group has. Multiple people use their expertise to perform some function and resolve issues.

9. b. Multi-disciplinary teams can work with many people handling different aspects of a situation. For substance abuse, a counselor may work alongside a halfway house for recovering addicts, a law enforcement department, and even clergy members to help a person who is suffering from substance abuse.

10. a. Cognitive behavior therapy focuses on looking at what causes a behavior to develop and analyzing the roots of a concern. As for the other options in this question, Gestalt therapy concentrates on a person's experiences. Adlerian therapy is understanding one's personality and how it can influence behavior. Person-centric therapy focuses on the individual person and does not consider outside influences.

11. c. The most important part of a support group is that it allows people to feel comfortable with one another. There is no need for aggression or medication. The people in the support group are encouraged to talk about their concerns with one another and find new and safe ways to cope.

12. d. REBT is about being confrontational. It concentrates on 'the shoulds, the oughts, and the musts' of desired behavior. REBT focuses on the philosophical and not the functional approach of cognitive therapy. This is in contrast to the collaborative nature of cognitive therapy (answers a, b, and c).

13. b. The struggle involved is the fourth step. A struggle will develop after a person identifies something, focuses on an idea, and then evaluates the needs that they might have. The connection occurs at the midway point as the person is ready to identify goals. The twelve steps, when followed in the proper order, ensure problems such as adjustment issues, depression, or anxiety can be resolved.

14. b. The test is to identify the signs of depression. The questions have varying values. For instance, the symptoms might be fatigue, a lack of interest, or thoughts of being a failure. This is not intended to determine if someone needs medication, although it may be required if it is determined that a person has an elevated risk of harm.

15. c. The key part of solution-focused coaching is to identify what is not working versus what is working. This may involve changing some things so that ideas are conveyed better. The solution to a problem is not always one that is directly related to the problem, nor is the solution something that might be easy to do.

16. b. An intervention is designed to identify harmful behaviors. This includes looking at ways to prevent a person's current problems from becoming worse than they already are. The person's mental state has to be considered and that the client is treated well with their best interests at the forefront of any actions.

17. b. The Imagery aspect of the BASIC ID theory considers the images that one might have in one's mind. This includes the negative thoughts, worries, or attitudes they have. Affect relates to the negative feelings, although this may not be related to the images in one's mind. Cognition is the degree of understanding of the thoughts or beliefs that one holds. Drugs are related to the negative effect on a person's body and mind.

18. a. Music therapy enhances one's mental functions. It can help a person to be calm so that they can converse easier. It can trigger the imagination and allow worries to dissipate and produce an atmosphere which allows rational thought.

19. d. All of the above. A task group can be convened where people will learn skills through participating in a project and supporting each other. A developmental group concentrates on reviewing how members of the group work side by side with one another. A support group focuses on how well members of the same group are willing to support each other with the difficult issues they may be working through as individuals.

20. d. The general purpose of grief counseling is to provide a positive voice for those who are dealing with significant emotional trauma or loss. It is to help the person grieving to come to terms with the event and give them an opportunity to put their feelings into words.

Research and Program Evaluation

1. As you review the results of someone's psychological profile, you would have to analyze the reliability and validity. The validity is a measure of how useful the test is. What would the reliability of the test be?

    a. Whether the person answered the questions correctly

    b. The simplicity of the results

    c. How consistent the test is

    d. Whether the person was willing to complete the test according to the rules

2. An item characteristic plot can be established when reviewing data. What would be plot involve?

    a. The types of responses people make

    b. How difficult the answer was

    c. The types of responses of one person versus the responses of the group

    d. How likely a person is to give an answer based on their ability

3. You notice that a client in your office is struggling with consistent fatigue and feelings that they are not performing well in life. You have a belief that people who have consistent fatigue and feelings of not performing suffer depression. Therefore, you would assume that the client has depression. In this case, what you are doing with the client?

    a. You are expressing syllogism.

    b. You are using quantitative research.

    c. You are working with a cross section of data to determine what the client is thinking.

    d. You are engaging in qualitative research.

4. You are working on a research project to identify how pregnant women think and communicate ideas. You might hear from some pregnant women in the study that they tire easily. What would you conclude from the statement of feeling fatigue in this study?

   a. This is an intervening variable.

   b. The fatigue may correlate to other issues.

   c. The struggles may not relate to fatigue.

   d. All pregnant women are likely to experience fatigue at some point.

5. You are participating in a research pilot project that involves reviewing how a medication might influence depression, if people can experience reduced depression symptoms when taking medication, or if the depression will worsen when taking the medication. You suspect some changes in the medication dosage might influence some of the results. What can be said about the medication doses?

   a. The drug being used may work as part of a larger control project.

   b. Not all people will respond to the medications being provided.

   c. The dosage is an independent variable.

   d. The dosage is a dependent variable.

6. What makes a Type I error in a test different from a Type II error?

   a. Type I is a false negative, while Type II is a false positive.

   b. Type I is something being correct without requiring change, while Type II involves the lack of a change causing something to be wrong.

   c. Type I is a false positive, while Type II is a false negative.

   d. There is a dramatic reporting error involved with whatever is being analyzed in the test.

7. A self-report personality test requires a person to fill in the results of a test on their own. This means that there is a possibility that a person will not tell the truth on a test. However, the testing involved may be beneficial in some way. What makes the self-report personality test useful even if the person involved is not going to answer every question truthfully?

    a. You will get an idea of what someone's personality might be like.

    b. You can see that a person displays several traits.

    c. You might notice how certain attitudes or beliefs might interact.

    d. There might be some kind of evolution in the functions and behaviors of the person being tested.

8. Phrenology is considered to be an outdated and obsolete practice, but it may still be used by some people. These include people who feel that the effort might result in a preview of what someone might be thinking. How can phrenology be used?

    a. To analyze how well individual parts of the cranium are shaped with an external review of the head shape

    b. To obtain an MRI to help with identifying any possible changes in brain activities

    c. To determine how someone might respond to certain questions or ideas

    d. All of the above

9. You want to identify the link in a study between the frequency of counseling visits versus the amount of change in a person's thoughts. What should you consider?

    a. Correlation between variables

    b. Cause and effect

    c. What happens when you adjust an independent variable

    d. How long it might take for a change to occur in the testing process

10. A study is being conducted to analyze how effective counseling is to help people who are recovering from drug addictions. Part of this study includes working with people who have been using medications to resolve their addictions. However, you are not aware of who has been using medications those who have not. What does this mean?

    a. The drugs being used are examined carefully to see what does and does not work.

    b. You might be asked to review how these drugs affect the addicted person.

    c. You could perform further interviews with the recovering addicts.

    d. You are blind to the results and are not aware of everything happening.

11. For what are you not going to use applied research?

    a. To study something

    b. To get answers to problems

    c. To receive a practical idea of what something can be used for

    d. All of the above

12. You can adopt a theory to determine what might be done when making a task work well. What would the theory for a study be?

    a. Guesses about what you believe is happening

    b. A discussion about something that you are trying to analyze

    c. Looking into something that a theory is trying to explain

    d. A series of data that you can use to make educated decisions

13. You can change the significance level in your test to change the risk of a Type I or Type II error developing. What will happen when a significant level is decreased?

    a. Both errors are less likely to occur.

    b. Both errors are more likely to occur.

c. A Type I error will be more likely, but a Type II error is less likely.

d. A Type I error will be less likely, but a Type II error is more likely.

14. You are testing people who are dealing with smoking addictions, and you want to determine what affect medications have on the addicted person. What can help you determine the possible effect of medications before the addicted persons in the test take the medications?

   a. You might use alternative methods of treatment.

   b. You can conduct interviews to determine which people in a study are responding to the interviews and other forms of support.

   c. You may administer a placebo to some of the people involved in the group.

   d. All of the above

15. What would happen if you attempted to use experimenter bias in your study?

   a. You are changing the types of participants who are entering the study in the hopes of making the test have positive results.

   b. You are changing how the research is to be done to facilitate a process that might be easier for you to complete.

   c. You are hiring different experimenters.

   d. You are adjusting the results of the test to produce the results you want.

16. How many samples can be used in your test?

   a. As many samples as you wish

   b. Only one

   c. Two to three to have general control

   d. Avoid using samples until you have tried the test on a few other people

Answers to Research and Program Evaluation

1. c. The reliability of the test is a measure of how consistent the results are. This might include looking at the results of the same test taken previously.

2. d. The item characteristic plot refers to the ability of a person to answer a question based on certain factors. The answers should be consistent throughout the entire process to confirm the reliability of the test.

3. a. Syllogism is a practice using assumptions based on prior data. The other solutions are not correct - cross-sectional research would require looking at many samples, qualitative research involves asking specific questions of each party in a situation, and quantitative research would use numerical data in the hopes of finding answers to the questions.

4. a. The fatigue in this example is an intervening variable. The variable directly influences the results. In this situation, the fatigue that a woman has might cause her to struggle to structure her thoughts or ideas. The fatigue might not necessarily correlate with other things happening in her situation. D is incorrect because there are no guarantees that a pregnant woman is going to experience fatigue.

5. c. The dosage of the medication is what is being changed in the test. Therefore, this is an independent variable. The dependent variable would be the results of the medication and how the client responds.

6. c. A Type I error is when a false positive occurs. In this case, the thing that has been measured or observed is true, but in reality, the concern is false. A Type II error is when something appears to be true in reality, but is perceived to be incorrect based on another test.

7. a. The test is designed to identify a single trend in one's personality. You might notice a very specific point in that person's attitudes or behaviors based on the answers that someone gives. You would not necessarily use this test to make generalizations about a client's personality or to predict future behavior.

8. a. The greatest concern surrounding phrenology is that while the practice is not invasive, it is often difficult to determine accuracy or reliability. Every person in the field will have different ideas of how well the practice works and what could be expected from the test.

9. a. The examination refers to the correction between the variables. These variables are the frequency of visits, the independent variable, and the results, which is the dependent variable.

10. d. The testing process is a blind test. This means that you do not know who has been using the medications. The test could also become a double-blind effort if the patients do not know that they are being given drugs or if they have been given placebos. For this question, you are participating in a single-blind study. The participant in the test may be the one who is blind, but in most cases the person conducting the test is blind.

11. a. You would not use applied research to study something new. Rather, you would use applied research to make discoveries.

12. d. A is incorrect because it relates to a hypothesis. The theory will have developed after you tested a hypothesis and discovered some solutions to a problem you are examining.

13. d. You will change the statistical significance of the study by making it easier for something to occur. You might change the original hypothesis of your study. The two types of errors that occur may also change in value. When the risk of one error decreases, the risk of the other error increases. In this case, the Type I error would not likely develop, but the Type II error is more likely to occur.

14. c. A placebo is a substance that is not going to influence responses. For instance, a sugar pill may be given to some people taking the test and given information that they are taking in medication to help them stop smoking. This group will be the control group. You may also notice a placebo effect, a condition where a person reports feeling better after taking a placebo, which should not change their condition at all.

15. d. The experimenter bias process occurs when the experimenter in the test is adjusting how the test works to alter the results.

16. a. You can use many samples for your test. You might use three sample groups if you have three results that you want to test for. You can also work with many sample groups based on the demographics. The number of samples will determine what you want to review and how much data you need to make the results significant.

Orientation and Ethics

1. A young child requires counseling to resolving a certain issue involving communicating with others. The child is unable to provide consent for services as the child is too young. What should you do to obtain consent?

    a. Ask the child's parents or legal guardians to provide consent.

    b. Ask other counselors for advice.

    c. Review the severity of the situation.

    d. Do nothing.

2. What are the rules regarding counseling clients with whom you have a prior romantic or sexual relationship?

    a. A professional board should be consulted before making the final decision.

    b. A person should not counsel someone who they have had a relationship with in the past.

    c. It is acceptable for someone to receive counseling services from a counselor they have had a relationship with.

    d. Sexual histories are not to be discussed.

3. You are conducting a group session, and you have some clients who might be sensitive to some topics. These include concerns surrounding any prior feelings one might have had. Part of this could be due to those people possibly having gone through events in the past that have impacted their ability to think clearly in certain situations. What is your role as the counselor in this situation?

    a. Expose the people to certain problems to desensitize them.

    b. Provide precautions to keep those people from being subjected to trauma.

    c. Allow the other people in the group to take over the conversations.

    d. Have those people who may be hurt by certain discussions go to another area.

4. An interruption has taken place during the treatment process. You are not going to be able to work with a client for a period of time for some reason. What should you do at this point?

    a. Allow the client to find someone else who can counsel them.

    b. Don't bother returning to the client if you cannot finish.

    c. Ask a substitute about other treatment opportunities including the use of medication to resolve concerns.

    d. Plan a convenient time when you can continue with counseling.

5. Information on your clients is intended to be private, but there might be times when you need to divulge that information to other people for specific reasons. When is it permissible to disclose information regarding a person you are counseling?

    a. When the person says it is alright to do so

    b. When a legal authority requests it

    c. When you feel there is an ethical need for doing so

    d. All of the above

6. You have a client who pays you for services, but that person has missed the last few payments. It is uncertain that the client is ever going to pay you for services in the past or for future services. What should you do about this client?

    a. Terminate the contract with the client, but provide a referral for other services.

    b. Terminate the contract and don't do anything else.

    c. Allow the person to continue to speak with you without paying for services.

    d. Continue to offer services, but hold back on some of your suggestions.

7. You can provide informed consent to your clients to help them manage the services you offer. Which of the following does not need to be included?

  a. The positives that come with what you are offering

  b. How you can be contacted in the event of an emergency

  c. Terms surrounding how you're going to charge the person for services

  d. Other services available for a person

8. You have been working in the field of counseling children, but you have recently expanded to include counseling services to elderly persons. What should you do when attempting to provide services for the elderly as well as children?

  a. You don't have do anything.

  b. You must have enough training and supervised experience before you can start offering services to the elderly.

  c. You need to advertise to the public to highlight what you are offering.

  d. You would need to ask co-workers about how to implement these services.

9. What should be done in the event that the counselor is unable to physically provide the services that a client needs? This includes when the counselor retires, terminates one's practice, becomes incapacitated, or dies suddenly.

  a. Nothing needs to happen; the clients should look for new services on their own.

  b. Clients should be referred to another professional for counseling.

  c. Any charges that were owed should be billed immediately and gathered by collection agencies.

  d. Any documentation that the counselor had should be released to everyone who had been receiving services.

10. You are getting a new office ready for your counseling services. You are considering a space that offers plenty of windows all around and a fake wall that features a one-way mirror. Is this type of space appropriate for your counseling practice?

    a. Yes

    b. No

    c. You'd have to cover the windows.

    d. You need to ensure licensed people monitor the situation to ensure fairness.

11. You might work with other counselors in your field to provide a thorough approach to care for your clients. What services should you request from other practitioners in other fields to handle your clients and their particular needs?

    a. You should be respectful of any people in other practices.

    b. You need to address some of the risks involved with some other practices.

    c. You should charge your clients a little extra for when they decide to use services that go beyond what you are already offering them.

    d. Avoid working with other professionals in different fields.

12. Although you need to ensure that you preserve confidentiality with your client, there might be times when you have to break the confidentiality agreement. Which of these situations is appropriate for doing so?

    a. When you need to warn other people about something serious involving your client

    b. When you are going to be out of town for an extended period of and you need to let others know about what is happening with your client

    c. When you feel that you need to talk with your client to delve deeper into some of the specific concerns that they have

    d. You do not need to second guess when you should break the agreement; you can do this at any time you feel is appropriate

13. Should a counselor question themselves as much as they question the client or other people in the field?

    a. Only if the situation demands to do so

    b. This is fine in all cases.

    c. Questioning the self produces doubt and should be avoided.

    d. The focus should be on the client.

14. You have a client who has been using speed and has been addicted to the drug for some time. The counseling involved is designed to help the addicted person resolve their drug addiction and to identify what can be done to resolve issues surrounding the damage caused by the addiction. What should be done in this case?

    a. Break the confidentiality agreement and talk with the proper authorities about the drug use.

    b. Be anonymous when talking to others about a client's drug use so you don't lose the client's trust in the process.

    c. Ask for details on where that person has acquired the illegal drugs so you can probe deeper into the situation.

    d. Avoid doing anything unless the person is threatening to harm themselves or another person.

15. What makes the value of your work as a counselor different from the ethics that you are required to follow?

    a. Value is what your services provide to your client and ethics are the rules you must follow to offer those services.

    b. Values will have specific boundaries.

    c. Everything is the same.

    d. You're predicting what you believe will happen when you use your values.

16. You are working with a large group of teens who are discussing concerns surrounding substance abuse. You are talking with them about their experiences with illegal substances and why they might be using them. What can you do when you allow the parents to contribute to the conversations?

    a. Allow the parents to attend the group sessions.

    b. Provide parenting classes surrounding issues involved with teen behavior.

    c. Provide a secretive space for parents to observe situations.

    d. All of the above

17. What should you do when deciding on a counseling approach that you wish to use with your clients?

    a. Provide services that are compatible with your personality.

    b. Be willing to offer services outside your personal beliefs or values.

    c. Prepare efforts that are unrelated to what you might be doing.

    d. Feel free to jump between different options as you see fit.

18. A person who is using your services has an extensive support group at their disposal, such as other family members, their manager at work, and a local clergyman. What should you do with all these people involved?

    a. Allow them to take part in the sessions.

    b. Keep them from attending the sessions.

    c. Interview each person before allowing them to take part in the sessions.

    d. Don't bother acknowledging these people's efforts.

19. A client has been working hard to be sober and has been sober for the last two years. One person who is related to that client tells you that the person has been drinking recently and that there are pictures on social media. What should you do about this situation?

    a. Acknowledge the issue but have that person tell your client to get help.

    b. Talk with your client to discuss the issue.

    c. Explain to the person who contacted you that you are unable to provide any suggestions.

    d. Allow that person to attend the next session that you hold with your client.

20. The Bradley Center v. Wessner Supreme Court case illustrates the duty to warn someone in authority about a patient or client who might be at risk of harming others. What does the court ruling state you need do?

    a. You must notify the authorities when someone might be at risk of harming others or themselves.

    b. Prior mental records should be consulted to determine how dangerous a person might be.

    c. A dangerous person should be held at a treatment facility to ensure they will not harm anyone.

    d. You need to protect anyone who may be identified as a possible victim.

21. Is it a good idea for you to attend the wedding or other major event involving one of your clients?

    a. Yes with no reservations.

    b. No

    c. Ask the person for permission.

    d. Check social media details.

22. Your professional services are being converted from working with therapeutic services to being evaluative in nature. What should you do regarding your clients?

   a. Provide full informed consent for the changes you propose.

   b. Allow your clients to share information about the changes with other family members.

   c. Do not let anyone know anything about what is going to happen.

   d. Ask your clients if they are in agreement for you to move to a different position.

23. What is not important if a counselor wants to be trusted by more people who might require services?

   a. A consistent social life

   b. Being friendly

   c. A desire to affirm people

   d. A sense of realism

24. What does the duty to warn specifically refer to?

   a. Informing people who want to take medications for resolving certain concerns

   b. Resolving concerns with experimental procedures that may not work as well as others

   c. How well you're going to manage social media contacts

   d. Protecting people who plan on possibly hurting themselves or others

25. Confidentiality refers to ensuring that information that is transferred during sessions with a client is kept private. What makes confidentiality important for counselors?

    a. It facilitates a sense of trust.

    b. The effort allows for a person to avoid having to tell others about the services one is providing.

    c. The practice might be something a client would look forward to.

    d. It becomes easier for clients to open up and share details about themselves.

26. Are there any particular demographics that could be considered when determining which counselor is going to be the most effective?

    a. Age

    b. Gender

    c. Social background

    d. Nothing

27. Counselors are often given gifts as thank-you tokens for the services received. What should you consider if you are given a gift by your client?

    a. Understand your motivation for receiving the gift.

    b. Consider the background of the client.

    c. Think about the general relationship that you have established with your client.

    d. All of the above

28. A third party group wants information on a client you are working with. What should you do?

    a. Ask how much money you would receive for this information.

    b. Ask the client they agree to give that person the information.

    c. Review any possible benefits the client might receive if you gave information.

    d. All of the above

29. A client says that she has HIV. What should you do in this case?

    a. Provide information on her condition to other third parties.

    b. Talk with her physical doctor for details.

    c. Ask her about how her condition has impacted her life and relationships.

    d. A and C

Answers to Orientation and Ethics

1. a. The most ethical thing to do is to ask the parents or legal guardians of the child to talk with you about the situation. The key is to allow enough people who are closely related to the person who requires help to have some input in the process.

2. b. The ACA Code of Ethics states that counselors are prohibited from engaging in counseling activities with those who they have had sexual relationships with in the past. There are concerns surrounding the close relationship between the two people and how that might potentially influence the process of offering to counsel to someone without having any biases or other issues.

3. b. You must provide precautions to ensure that people are not negatively impacted by the things you are talking about. These include concerns surrounding any physical or emotional trauma. You also have the option to ask if they wish to discuss these things.

4. d. The best solution you have is to ensure you let the client resume counseling sessions with you soon. You'll have to talk about when you are expected to return to work and what the client can do in the meantime. It doesn't matter the cause of the interruption. You should not abandon a client that you are counseling, but you could make suitable arrangements for another counselor to continue in your absence if that is agreeable with your client.

5. d. Everything that is discussed in counseling sessions should be kept confidential at all times. There might be instances where you need to release information on the client in question, such as where the client gives consent to release the information when a legal authority is asking for the information. This may include a hospital, police station, or other authority that needs the information for analysis and for confirming concerns surrounding public issues. If your client is at risk of harming themselves or others you should inform someone in authority.

6. a. You have the right to terminate a person's contract for services, but you must ensure that you provide an appropriate referral. This includes allowing the person to contact another professional who can provide service. You should ensure that the person receives the support they need well in the future. You may also consider C as an option, but you should review your financial concerns as well. D is not an answer as you should still ensure that you provide the best services you can even if there is some concern surrounding the relationship between you and the client. It is also recommended that you avoid trying to force payment as that might make it harder for the person to trust your services.

7. d. Although you have the option to provide your client with details on other services you can provide, you do not necessarily have to offer this to a client. You should ensure that your services are the most appropriate for the client. You should not feel obligated to provide a person with details on other services available to them.

8. b. Counselors have the right to expand into any particular specialty areas of practice. However, a counselor would have to complete certification and training before offering services in a particular field. You would also have to speak with any clients you wish to work with about any changes you are contemplating.

9. b. An appropriate plan should a counselor be unable to provide regular services to their clients. For instance, you might contact a professional organization to ensure that your clients can find other services.

10. b. It is never appropriate to have a secret room or space where there's a two-way mirror (sometimes called a one-way glass) used for observation. Avoid having a window installed where people from outside can view your clients.

11. a. You need to provide the client with the final choice as to use other services. The patient should have the freedom to consider and approve of the treatment being offered.

12. a. The confidentiality agreement dictates that you cannot provide any details about a client to others unless there is a legitimate life-threatening concern.

13. b. It is not only appropriate for you to question your work as a counselor, but it is strongly recommended. You can review how your client is responding to treatment and decide what can be done to resolve certain problems that might be occurring. You should analyze your ability to handle a patient's needs when managing various mental or emotional concerns.

14. d. D is correct because it ensures a patient is kept comfortable and will not be judged in the treatment process. A is incorrect because a confidential agreement applies unless there is a threat that your client may be in danger of self-harm or of harming someone else. The other choices are incorrect as you are to ensure privacy for the client.

15. d. Ethics will dictate the boundaries of your work, not the values. Your values will support what you feel will happen. You will have to continue to offer services based on ethical considerations. You must not be judgmental if you experience problems and the results are different from your values.

16. b. You should allow the parents to learn about any issues surrounding their teen's behavior. You must ensure the parents do not take part in the sessions and cannot be allowed to view the sessions. The information you provide outside of a session may help a parent understand certain concerns that their kids are dealing with.

17. a. Erickson states that it is easier for clinicians to provide services when they understand how their services compare with their personality types. This may require extra training and analysis on your part to figure out what style of counseling you should offer.

18. a. You should allow the support group that a person has to attend the sessions you are providing. The support group can help a client recognize what they can do to help themselves.

19. a. You should not use a client's social media profiles to your advantage. Any use of social media to find details might be interpreted as being inappropriate or a violation of privacy. The best thing to do is to listen to the person telling you about your client and to recommend a private intervention to resolve the issue. You do have the option to allow that person to attend a session unless the client approves.

20. c. The counselor will need to ensure a person is kept in custody if they are at risk of harming another person or themselves. Answer D focuses on Tarasoff vs. The Regents of the University of California, a case stating that a counseling group should care for the intended victim of some event and provide care to prevent harm from occurring. Answer B refers to Jablonski by Pahls vs. the United States, a case stating that a counselor may review medical records if a person is threatening harm to anyone so as to potentially identify any possible concerns that might influence one's mental capacity.

21. c. The ACA Code of Ethics does not state that you are not allowed to maintain a positive working relationship with a client outside of the standard sessions. However, you must contact the client to determine if they are willing to have you attend an event. When going to such an event, you may risk concerns surrounding informed consent, documentation, and supervision. You will have to ensure that the judgment that the client has is not impaired or influenced because of your presence at a particular event. Also, you should avoid providing services to your client until you are on the clock and in the proper place where you can provide service.

22. a. You have the full right to move your focus from one segment to the next. But before you do that, you must provide informed consent to your clients. This

allows your client to refuse services if they so choose. Inform your clients before you implement changes so they are prepared.

23. a. Your social life should not be a factor in your work regardless of how active it is. There is nothing wrong with having a social life when working as a counselor. Having a strong social life is valuable as it lessens stress and might positively influence your work. At the same time, you need to be friendly, work with a sense of realism, and affirm your clients to enable them to move forward.

24. d. The duty to warn is a practice that protects people who might pose a danger to themselves or to other people. You might have to contact other professionals to express your concerns.

25. d. Although all of these options are useful, D is the best choice. You may obtain more information from a client if a confidentiality agreement is in place.

26. d. It is uncertain as to what demographics would contribute to the best and most effective counseling service.

27. d. There are no particular rules in the ACA Code of Ethics stating that you specifically have to avoid accepting gifts from clients. However, you should think about the monetary value of the gift and the reasoning for why you would accept a gift or why the client might have wanted to give you this gift. You could also review a person's background, as some cultures approve of providing gifts to those who offer the most valuable service.

28. b. You should not consider anything you or your client might earn when looking at a third party's offer for details. The client should have the final say about whether or not their information is to be shared with other parties.

29. a. and c. The woman's HIV diagnosis might be something that could have influenced her life in many ways including changing her relationships. But you have the right to divulge information about communicable diseases to third parties if necessary. This includes cases of HIV/AIDS and other conditions that can be transferred to other parties. You will have to review the laws in your state surrounding the disclosure of information about transmittable diseases to third parties.

Test #2

Human Growth

1. Over time, a person will move to a state of relativistic thinking. What does this concept mean?

    a. Things may be easier to distinguish between right and wrong.

    b. It is easier to give an answer based on a very specific situation.

    c. The answer one makes can be changed at any time as something happens.

    d. Any choices one makes might not actually matter.

2. Piaget states that after a few years, a child will explore the concept of reversibility. This occurs in the concrete stage of development. What does the concept of reversibility mean?

    a. Any decisions one makes are to be set in stone.

    b. Old actions can be undone.

    c. Certain things might be heavier or lighter than they appear.

    d. A person's mental capacity can move in reverse if not handled well.

3. Erikson states that after a while, a person might experience the following:

    a. Identity crisis

    b. Helplessness

    c. Inferiority complex

    d. Positive thoughts

4. Erikson states people will go through many stages in life, but the last stage appears when the person reaches 65 years of age. At this point in life, a person might have gone through everything one could experience in life, which leads to the following internal debate:

    a. Integrity or despair

    b. Intimacy or isolation

    c. Industry or inferiority

    d. Generativity or stagnation

5. What did Vygotsky decide about the concept of proximal development?

    a. Performance is based on how well a person studies.

    b. Performance is based on compatibility.

    c. A person's interest influences results.

    d. Work routines are hard to predict unless there is a sense of consistency.

6. At what age is a person most likely to conform to their peers' activities?

    a. Age 6

    b. Age 14

    c. Age 25

    d. Age 40

7. Freud states that every dream that a person has at any age will have some kind of a latent meaning to it. What would this mean?

    a. Literal meaning

    b. Figurative meaning

    c. Hidden meaning

    d. Sexual considerations involved

8. What can be said about suicide rates among people?

    a. They tend to be higher among older people.

    b. They tend to be higher among younger people.

    c. Suicide rates are consistent among all people of every age.

    d. It is difficult to analyze the rates of occurrence according to age.

9. Attachment is a concept originated by Freud that entails how well a person might work to be attached to someone. What can be said about attachment?

    a. It is more likely to develop among younger people.

    b. This is a concept that can occur among all people regardless of age.

    c. An attachment has a strong sexual nature linked to it.

    d. You can never tell how attached someone might be to something unless you ask that person about it.

10. What can be said about development?

    a. There are limits as to how long it might take for something to develop.

    b. It is hard to determine what might occur.

    c. This occurs from conception onward.

    d. This starts at birth.

11. Severe trauma in a child's life can cause the child's development to become significantly restricted according to Freud. What does this mean for the overall psychosexual evolution of the child?

    a. A child will skip a stage in the developmental process.

    b. The child will move backward in developmental.

    c. The child will remain at one developmental stage.

    d. All of the above.

12. What can be said about instinctual responses that people might experience?

    a. These are normal for people to have.

    b. It is easier for men to show instinctual behavior than women.

    c. People who are supported by their parents will have a better chance of developing the proper instinctual behaviors.

    d. All of the above

Answers to Human Growth

1. b. Relativistic thinking entails how a correct answer can come about based on something that a person is thinking. The conceit is that there are many ways how people can review the world. The correct answer should be relative to what is happening in a situation and what should be done to resolve any issues that might develop. This is different from dualistic thinking, which is a process where a person identifies the difference between right and wrong. Many answers might be inflexible, thus making it harder for you to make a proper decision.

2. b. Reversibility states that old actions can be reversed. These include actions that might be complicated or difficult to predict.

3. a. Erikson states a person can develop an identity crisis when they are confused over their role in life and how well their behaviors or attributes manage that role well. The challenge that comes from the identity crisis can be frustrating to many, but it does not necessarily cause a person to become helpless, nor is it going to trigger an inferiority complex that Adler suggests.

4. a. The oldest stage in Erikson's theory of psychosocial development states that a person will feel either integrity over their actions throughout life or despair over the lack of results in life after the age of 65.

5. b. Proximal development involves familiarity and compatibility when looking at how well things work. A person has to be compatible with the person who is teaching the content to be useful and memorable. There may also be an influence surrounding the general way how a person learns new things.

6. b. The desire for a person to conform will be the greatest in a person's early teens. At this age, a person might be interested in what others are doing and might be willing to adopt certain personality traits or attitudes so that they are accepted by the group.

7. c. It is believed there are hidden meanings involved with everything that someone might be doing. The hidden meanings in one's work can be anything surrounding challenges in what one might be thinking or the attitudes that a person holds about others.

8. a. People who are older in age are at a higher risk of committing suicide. The reason for this is older people might be too depressed for various reasons. People may be depressed because they are not as healthy or they have fewer peers. Younger might also be at risk of having suicidal thoughts or actions if they don't know what roles they have in society or they have been abused by their peers or family members.

9. a. The attachment involves how a person might be very closely linked to certain things in the early stages of one's life. In particular, a person might be attached to their mother during the earliest years of life. Although older persons may develop attachments to various items, their attachments to things are not as strong as in the early years.

10. c. Psychologists tend to review development as something that starts from conception onward. Many prenatal factors might be factors for how a person develops. These include some of the more common risks that might influence an unborn child including smoking or alcohol use during pregnancy.

11. c. Fixation is a concern that might develop when severe trauma occurs. Fixation develops when a child is unable to move between developmental stages. In other cases, the child might not want to leave a stage out of fear of what might happen. The child's emotions can be severely restricted. Any physical or cognitive functions that a child can handle will continue to move forward, although the emotional state of the child will likely remain at the stage when trauma was experienced.

12. a. Instinctual behaviors are ones that people are going to learn on their own and naturally develop. These behaviors are consistent among people of the same culture and are consistent regardless of age, gender, or other factors.

Social and Cultural Diversity

1. Regardless of the person's culture or to what society someone belongs, Freud and Lorenz both argue that every human has an instinct for which of the following?

    a. Fighting

    b. Loving

    c. Working

    d. Planning

2. What can be noticed when a multicultural counselor engages in providing services?

    a. A person has a strong bias towards people of one particular culture.

    b. A person only works with solutions surrounding certain things involved with one's activities.

    c. The counselor has a culture that is different from the person who needs assistance.

    d. None of the above

3. You are planning to diagnose a client who has a different culture. What should you do in this situation?

    a. Identify some of the specifics surrounding the client's culture.

    b. Be direct with the client.

    c. Determine if a person can comprehend the services you provide.

    d. Try to postpone discussions.

4. What do social learning experts believe about people and how they behave within cultures?

    a. It may be difficult for people in some cultures to comprehend some of the diagnoses they might have been given.

    b. People are only willing to ask for counseling if they really feel this way.

    c. Feelings of aggression are learned.

    d. People are always going to be attached to specific persons in their lives.

5. What does contextualism mean?

    a. You have to look at multiple cultures to understand how different ideas might develop and how people may think.

    b. It may be difficult to ensure accuracy when looking at the cultural values of a client.

    c. There is a context surrounding every theory you are going to use when diagnosing a client.

    d. You have to analyze behavior based on the context of one's culture.

6. Those who are poor might be more likely to engage in which of the following behaviors?

    a. Apathy

    b. Aggression

    c. Pleasure

    d. Positivity

7. Culture is considered to be a normative concept. The rules and ideas within a culture are responsible for behavior. Which of the following applies to the normative values associated with a culture?

    a. Every culture offers unique norms that are similar in a few ways.

    b. No one can ever truly learn every single aspect surrounding a culture.

    c. Culture has a series of conduct standards that must be followed.

    d. Customs are not included in culture.

8. General norms dictate the particular conduct that one would engage in. A cultural norm will be different in which of the following ways?

    a. Involves the proper actions of people

    b. Does not relate to expectations

    c. Can be flexible in nature

    d. Will not be concerning to most individuals

9. Are children in one part of the world likely to become more vocal or mentally advanced versus children from another part of the world?

    a. Yes

    b. No

    c. Only in the southern hemisphere

    d. Depending on the continent the child lives

10. Ethnocentrism is a belief that some cultures have regarding how they might have evolved. What does this concept mean?

    a. One's culture is superior to all others

    b. Every race is the same

    c. Some people have better genetics than others

    d. All of the above

11. Of the following, which type of person do all cultures believe to be the most popular?

    a. A person who has strong social skills

    b. A person who places values of one's own culture above all others

    c. Anyone who has a good fashion sense

    d. Someone who is not going to be judgmental of other people

Answers to Social and Cultural Diversity

1. a. The instincts that people have exhibiting behavior can influence the mind. Freud suggests such instincts could be sexual and aggressive tendencies. Lorenz bases his belief in instinct on the concept of fish attacking things even when their main targets are avoided. Humans may not be as aggressive as animals, but their urges can be noticed regardless of where one might be in life or what one's background is.

2. c. A multicultural counselor will need to be someone who understands many cultures. This includes identifying many opportunities for helping people based on their lives and cultures.

3. a. Cultural awareness is important for all counselors to have. It is important to review the perspectives a culture has on certain conditions when discussing the needs that a client has.

4. c. Observational learning often involves looking at how people respond to certain situations. People are likely to learn about aggression and other behaviors.

5. d. Every concept or value in counseling will have some special meaning depending on the context. Contextualism refers to when something might have a unique meaning based on how a person understands certain values.

6. b. Aggression is an issue that develops in cultures where money is not easily available. As a result, people often take out their frustrations on others because they feel they have been wronged in some way.

7. c. Conduct standards must include details on how well people are to behave and act around others.

8. a. Cultures could be interpreted as a series of norms. Cultural norms are extended expectations for how people behave what they might contribute to their social groups.

9. b. All children develop in the same way based on the words that they learn and how well they can vocalize. The timeframe should be the same for all children, although the rules for how they are to behave can vary based on where they come from and what behaviors are acceptable.

10. a. Ethnocentrism argues that one's group is always going to be more superior to others in the world. While there are no arguments involved based on race or background, ethnocentrism argues that one's cultural values dictate how they live and other ideas are not appreciated.

11. a. Social skills are critical in all cultures. People who know how to convey ideas and thoughts will easily get along with other people. This is why some people with various cultures might seek counseling. They might want to learn how they can be better communicators without embarrassing themselves or being seen as people who are not as valuable as others in society.

Helping Relationships

1. What makes cognitive therapy different from other forms of therapy when helping people with their relationships?

    a. It analyzes dreams.

    b. It reviews what a person is thinking.

    c. It reviews the actions that a person is engaging in.

    d. The practice requires extensive medication.

2. For cognitive therapy to work, a proper sense of understanding of the patient is necessary. What should be used when determining the general background of the client?

    a. Prior relationships

    b. Attitudes towards others

    c. Fears about things

    d. Relationship of beliefs to current problems

3. The rational emotive behavior therapy states that some events may result in certain emotions and those emotions can be unhealthy or healthy. For instance, a negative event can trigger negative emotions. What could potentially happen based on a person's belief?

    a. A rational belief can reverse the negative emotion to a positive one.

    b. An irrational belief can cause a negative emotion to become irrational.

    c. A rational belief prompts further worry about the negative emotion causing that feeling to become worse.

    d. An irrational belief can prompt someone to think about whether or not the original event is significant.

4. Reality therapy supports a healthy relationship between two people. This includes determining whether the people are receiving what they want out of the relationship. What is the most important consideration of reality therapy to be used?

   a. Determining how people are incorporating past lessons in their lives

   b. Determining how responsible the people are in the relationship

   c. Determining the punishments that are meted out

   d. Identifying how happy people are

5. You are currently helping a child who has had behavioral issues in the past. The child is being rewarded for engaging in specific behaviors. The child receives a more significant reward for every couple of positive behaviors that they display. The reinforcement schedule that is evident here is which one of the following?

   a. Variable ratio

   b. Variable interval

   c. Fixed ratio

   d. Fixed interval

6. The concept of shaping may be used in various situations to change how people may behave or act in society. What is shaping?

   a. Impersonating the behaviors that others are engaging in

   b. Identifying how groups may behave and seeing what roles may contribute to how those groups evolve and thrive

   c. Learning behaviors in brief steps

   d. Determining the conditions in which certain behaviors produce the best results

7. A person is nodding one's head when listening to you. That person is also say "yes" or "okay" many times while you are talking. That individual is not directly responding to any other prompts from you. The things that a person is doing, in this case, are examples of which of the following?

    a. Clarification

    b. Reflection

    c. Exploration

    d. General lead

8. An older woman who has dementia is talking with you. She keeps on referring to you by a different name. This may be the name of someone who was close to her in her life. What should you do in this case?

    a. Say that you are her counselor and that you are not the person she thinks you are.

    b. Ignore her and giving a gentle chuckle over the situation.

    c. Acknowledge that you are the person she thinks you are.

    d. Ask her to stop calling you by that name.

9. You are counseling a client who has gone through a divorce, and you learn that they begin dating other people about three months after the divorce was finalized. You start to feel upset about the situation because it reminds you of a situation in your past. The issue is a sign of which of the following?

    a. Transference

    b. Countertransference

    c. Being doubtful

    d. Finding new information

10. What could cause transference to develop with a client?

    a. Anxiety surrounding a situation

    b. A lack of contact with someone

    c. Certainty over one's personality

    d. A desire to help

11. What would happen in an incidence of movement complementarity?

    a. One person talks and the second talks about something that adds to what the first person introduced.

    b. One person talks and the second nods their head.

    c. One person talks and the second talks about something completely different.

    d. Both parties are silent as they think about how they are going to interact with each other.

12. What would be the best thing for someone to do when they focus on cognitive therapy processes to help a client?

    a. Allow the person to identify and modify their thoughts.

    b. Allow the person to review their emotions and to clarify those feelings.

    c. Let the person's emotions be revealed and determine what can be done to resolve them.

    d. Avoid enabling a person to do something.

13. The act of rational emotive behavior therapy may work with different types of data. An action that requires determining the content and ideas in a situation can be called which of the following?

    a. Logical dispute

    b. Empirical dispute

    c. Rational alternative belief

    d. Functional dispute

14. Eye movement desensitization and reprocessing, or EMDR, is a practice that identifies eye movements. What is the best use of EMDR?

    a. To see if a person is paying attention to you

    b. To understand whether or not a person is comprehending the ideas or concepts that you are presenting

    c. To determine how a person responds to particular stimuli

    d. To identify how a person handles negative information

15. Freud and Jung had different theories about the causes of behaviors in relationships. While they both felt that past experiences are likely to influence the behaviors, what makes their theories different?

    a. Freud focuses on external factors, while Jung concentrates on internal factors

    b. Jung concentrates mainly on sexual desires, while Freud avoids sex in his discussions

    c. Jung considers future aspirations, while Freud concentrates on things that happened in one's childhood

    d. Freud feels that repressed desires could be critical factors, while Jung does not believe that those desires are so important

16. Which feelings are the most important to consider when conveying those feelings?

    a. Past

    b. Present

    c. Future

    d. All are important

17. Which of the following is true about the superego?

    a. This is the second part of the person's mind to develop.

    b. It develops based on pleasures.

    c. It controls the responses produced by the id.

    d. It regulates a person's personality.

18. A therapist introduces a client to services by explaining what will take place during a therapy session. This includes discussing the fact that the client is responsible for solving their own problems. The sessions will focus on positive thinking. What type of therapy approach is the therapist describing?

    a. Person-centered therapy

    b. Gestalt therapy

    c. Cognitive therapy

    d. Analytic therapy

19. What does Freud believe the goal of therapy should be?

    a. To allow the unconscious mind to control the thoughts one has

    b. To force a person to control information that the ego has repressed

    c. To hide repressed thoughts

    d. To help people to find ways to avoid unhappiness as much as possible

20. Which part of Jungian treatment is the display of strong emotions?

   a. Catharsis

   b. Elucidation

   c. Education

   d. Transformation

21. Considering the psychoanalytic theory, what makes transactional analysis unique?

   a. The analysis focuses on the existential points of how a person behaves.

   b. The analysis considers the cognitive considerations of behavior.

   c. It is a more humanistic theory of behavior.

   d. Solutions may be easy to develop based on the analysis.

22. Eric Berne developed transactional analysis as a means of understanding how a person may respond to different stimuli and concepts. What was the main belief that Berne had when forming this analytical standard?

   a. Many ideas may be organized in a single line to identify what someone might be thinking.

   b. General attitudes surrounding one's thoughts may not change much.

   c. A person has the ability to deflect one's thoughts and emotions onto other people.

   d. People can re-experience thoughts and emotions.

23. Holden states that there are many factors that can keep a person from developing in a healthy way. These include concerns that will keep a person from feeling positive about themselves. Which of the following is not one of the factors that may hinder a person's general development?

    a. Inexperience that causes a person's ability to learn to be minimal

    b. Cognitive immaturity

    c. Exposure to other people

    d. Genetic factors

24. What does Skinner's operant reinforcement theory state?

    a. The frequency of one's behavior is influenced by the events following this behavior.

    b. A person's behavior may be influenced by the opinions that others have of that behavior.

    c. Social norms may be a factor in determining the behaviors of a person.

    d. It may be difficult for people to decide what they are supposed to do with their lives unless they ask others.

25. What is classical conditioning used for?

    a. Helping a person to stop smoking

    b. Allowing a person to learn to drive

    c. Giving a person ways to spend money

    d. Resolving certain marital disputes

26. Applied behavior analysis is a part of behavior therapy that focuses on what point?

    a. How cognitions can change the emotions one might have

    b. Conditioning to change behaviors

    c. Understanding the behavioral and cognitive considerations that may develop

    d. How environmental events may influence one's behaviors

27. What is the first step in the behavioral therapy process?

    a. Conceptualize the problem

    b. Decide on a strategy for managing one's life

    c. Roleplay

    d. Review the dreams that a person has about the problem in question

28. What is behavior therapy designed to do for you?

    a. Help analyze your thoughts

    b. Control the feelings of perfection

    c. Get rid of unwanted behaviors

    d. Be able to communicate with other people

29. What is the main focus of reality therapy?

    a. Reviewing the troubles encountered in studying

    b. Planning good relationships with other people

    c. Considering the here and now

    d. Correcting any unrealistic thoughts

30. William Glasser argues that there are two general needs that a person has. Which of the following answers is one of the two basic needs in life?

    a. Respect

    b. Connection

    c. Understanding

    d. Love

31. What should be considered first in reality therapy?

    a. Evaluation

    b. Wants

    c. Directions

    d. Any of the answers a., b., or c.

32. Multimodal therapy is a form of behavioral therapy developed by Lazarus that identifies some of the problems that may develop. The focus of this therapy involves:

    a. Modeling

    b. Context

    c. Influences

    d. Fears

33. There are many archetypes that can develop when understanding how relationships might develop. What is the most powerful of these archetypes?

    a. Persona

    b. Warrior

    c. Anima

    d. Shadow

34. The paradoxical theory of change can be emphasized by which of the following?

    a. Good things will happen in your life if you stop trying and let events flow naturally.

    b. Happiness is not easy to control unless you have an idea of what you want in life.

    c. The more you try to be someone that you are not, the more you will stay the same.

    d. You might struggle with other people if they are not similar to you or you are not aware of how they might behave in different ways.

35. What can be said about the concept of being ready to change?

    a. It is a flexible aspect of life.

    b. This is a fixed point in life that cannot be changed.

    c. You may manage some of the functions in your life with this concept.

    d. You are not going to feel motivated when you are not ready to change.

36. A client that you are working with has come in late for their session. He says that he is late because he does not have a car and it is difficult for him to find rides. You could suggest taking the bus, but he says that he's afraid of what would happen if people saw him doing this. You talk with him about whether this belief is valid, and then you encourage him to take a bus ride to and from certain places. This includes introducing himself to a few people on the bus. What is this type of activity an example of?

    a. Desensitization

    b. Role-playing

    c. Shame-attacking

    d. None of the above

Answers to Helping Relationships

1. b. Cognitive therapy focuses on identifying how people think about certain things. Instead of looking at emotions, a person's attitudes and thoughts are studied to identify any possible concerns that might have developed. The goal is to determine why someone feels a certain way. The term comes from cognition, which relates to thought.

2. d. Although different feelings that a person has could be analyzed, the key is to link those feelings to their activities. This includes reviewing the attitudes that someone has surrounding specific behaviors or thoughts that they have. A general review of current events in one's life and the things that someone is doing based on actions or attitudes can be used.

3. b. The rationality of the belief will trigger the intensity of the emotion that one feels following an event. A rational belief that occurs during a negative event will not keep the emotion from being negative, but the person will at least have a sense of realism and control over what one is thinking at a given time. An irrational belief surrounding that negative event will cause the person in question to become even more worried and possibly more frustrated about the situation.

4. b. Responsibility is critical to ensure that a person is psychologically sound and strong with regards to what one is thinking or feeling. Reality therapy focuses not on past events or on any negative feelings, but rather on how responsible people are for their actions. People are not punished in reality therapy, nor are they going to undergo extensive assessments or investigations. Rather, the people will be tested based on what might develop and how they might make the proper changes in their lives.

5. c. A fixed ratio states that reinforcement is given after a person participates in enough positive activities. In the question here, the child will receive a greater reward after engaging in enough positive behaviors. The reward should be provided after the child has proven an ability to engage in certain actions. The fixed schedule is where a person will receive a greater reward after a varying number of attempts or behaviors.

6. c. Shaping is a gradual process. A person will learn new behaviors and ideas through a series of conditioned steps. Those steps are to be followed if a person wishes to be more productive or efficient in what they are doing. Shaping may develop at any point in one's life, although it is particularly noticeable among children.

7. d. A general lead refers to when someone is acknowledging what someone is saying or doing. The lead may be verbal or non-verbal. The lead identifies what someone is thinking. A clarification would require a verbal response asking to confirm something that a person just said. Reflection is summarizing the ideas that were introduced. Exploration would also be verbal and would involve trying to delve deeper into the things that someone is talking about.

8. a. When speaking with older persons with a degenerative disease you can say that you are not that person, but that you have a different name and that you are their counselor. You should not force the person to stop calling you by a different name or ignore the situation. The goal is to be gentle and to help orient a patient without being disruptive or harsh.

9. b. Countertransference occurs when you start to remember things in your life based on what you are learning from someone else. In this example, your frustration with the client is reflective of how you've tried in your past to change your attitudes.

10. a. Anxiety can trigger frustration or worry. This may cause a person to become vulnerable and more likely to go through transference. The act of transference is more likely to occur with who have experienced vulnerability. Other issues involved may include regular contact with others directly associated with one's feelings or personality issues where a person has a borderline personality.

11. b. A complementarity action occurs when the two people in the conversation pair their movements accordingly. One person will talk, and the other will nod their head to acknowledge what is being said. The complementarity of certain actions may influence positive attitudes and behaviors. This is different from movement synchrony where the two people interacting with one another act the same way. Movement dyssynchrony would display nonverbal behaviors.

12. a. Cognitive therapy is about looking at a person's thoughts. This includes identifying and evaluating thought patterns. Some changes may be made to those thoughts to ensure the thoughts are sensible while also keeping thought distortion from being a threat.

13. b. All four of the answers are vital parts of REBT. The empirical dispute is the most important part to follow in that the dispute is based on the collection of evidence and ideas. Logical disputes focus less on evidence and more on reasoning and understanding a situation on one's own. A rational alternative would involve an alternative belief that may help explain or change a thought or action.

14. d. The EMDR process identifies what a person might do when paying attention to negative stimuli. EMDR works particularly well in cases where a person has post-traumatic stress disorder and a certain trigger has to be identified to understand the concern. EMDR may also work for anxiety, depression, substance abuse, and other concerns that may trigger negative feelings and thoughts.

15. c. Freud believes behaviors in childhood can influence their behaviors and thoughts as an adult. Jung concentrates mainly on prior experiences and future aspirations or desires. Freud focuses on sexual gratification when it comes to the person's libido while Jung looks at how libido influences many behaviors. D is also incorrect because both parties feel that repressed memories are essential in many ways; Jung concentrating on how the unconscious mind stores repressed memories and Freud believes the unconscious mind focuses on individual-specific desires.

16. b. The present is the most important consideration as it reveals the feelings that one has right now. These are the feelings that need to be resolved to make a situation easier in order to make proper decisions and have sensible ideas in the future.

17. d. The superego helps manage one's personality. The superego reviews how personality evolves and develops. This includes looking at what might cause a person to think positively or to have rational thought. A is not correct because the superego is the last part of the mind to develop. B is also incorrect as the id evolves through the desires that one has. C is wrong as well, as the ego is what is responsible for suppressing the random desires that the id holds.

18. a. Person-centered therapy is a concept introduced by Rogers to help people understand how their relationships are evolving with the client leading the way. The counselor is not going to directly tell the client what should be done to solve a problem. Rather, the client's concerns are analyzed with friendly attitudes and thoughts to producing a sense of positivity and rapport with the client.

19. b. Freud argues that therapy is designed to help people understand reality and to help the ego manage repressed information. This is to help people to acknowledge their realities and to show that they understand the concerns they have. A is incorrect because Jung states that therapy helps to heal a person's attitude by allowing the unconscious to complete its job and to handle what it has been doing as necessary.

20. a. The four stages listed are in chronological order from A to D. A is the first part, as it allows a person to express their emotions. Elucidation would follow as a practice to identify the symptoms that come with one's feelings and how these

beliefs are to be studied. Education would involve looking into ways to manage one's feelings and to determine what a person can do to mature and to become a stronger individual. The transformation occurs at the end when the person allows for self-dialogue to have a better understanding of the feelings that they have and how to resolve any issues surrounding those feelings.

21. c. The humanistic approach to psychoanalytic theory focuses on the realistic things surrounding one's life. The unconscious mind is not a focus, although this may be considered. The humanistic approach concentrates of reviewing a person's emotional health and social relationships. The general approach does put in a small emphasis on parental messages and on how a child develops in the early years.

22. d. Berne believes in people can re-experience the emotions and thoughts that they've had in the past. In addition, people can experience these rather vividly. The vivid nature of the experiences can be identical to what they experienced in the past.

23. c. The exposure that one has to other people may not be as much of a factor in inhibiting one's general emotional growth. In some cases, a person may not have the proper exposure to ideas of values that may help with improving upon one's work. But in other cases, a person might feel uncomfortable with the ideas that are being conveyed by others. Other people are not necessarily going to impact the mind as much as the ability of a person to try and limit the influences that those people might impose on someone else.

24. a. The operant reinforcement theory states that a person would try to produce different feelings about things that they experience. Although the other answers could be considered, the theory from Skinner suggests that people will do things that are appreciated and supported more often than not.

25. a. Classical conditioning is an idea developed by Pavlov to change behaviors. A response to an external stimuli many times can produce the response without the stimuli.

26. d. The applied behavioral analysis identifies environmental events that can influence one's behavior. These include events like any changes in the environment including changes in the people they regularly associate with. A is an example of cognitive behavior therapy. B is an example of neo-conditioning, a practice where a person's behaviors or responses may be conditioned. C is the social learning theory, a practice of understanding the behaviors based on various cognitive factors that will influence one's behavior.

27. a. Conceptualization is a review of the nature of the situation. The context of the behavior is then reviewed to determine the concern. B is the second step in behavioral therapy. In this case, the new strategies being planned will help control any conditions that one might have developed.

28. c. Behavior therapy is used to eliminate unhealthy and unappealing behaviors. Behavior therapy can be applied for cases of trying to stop smoking or improve study skills.

29. c. Reality therapy does not involve things that happened in the past. Rather, reality therapy concentrates on the changes that can be made in one's life to improve behavior.

30. a. Relatedness refers to love and respect involves having a sense of worth. Although the other options are possible, these are dependent on relatedness and respect.

31. d. Reality therapists argue that there are no set rules for the order to manage one's ideas. Therapists work with the WDEP acronym, which stands for: wants, direction, doing, evaluation, and planning. These can be applied in many ways, as there are no standards. However, many people might consider evaluation to be the beginning step.

32. b. Multimodal therapy applies to any behaviors and any influences that a person has. The social learning theory and cognitive therapy theory are both applied when identifying ways how one's behaviors develop and how they might change.

33. d. The shadow is not only the most powerful of these archetypes, but it is the riskiest and most dangerous. The shadow can appear in dreams and may be used as a servant in one's relationships, although it may also be a part of one's persona. The shadow is the opposite gender of the person who is noticing this aspect of one's life. The shadow is a part of one's identity that is not displayed in public, and it is not always something that people are consciously aware of when they are behaving in some ways.

34. c. The paradoxical theory of change states that a person needs to accept who they are and change will occur when that happens and not if that person tries to become what he is not. Changes cannot happen by being coerced or influenced by someone else.

35. a. The readiness to change is reflective of one's ability to change things in life and to make things work for them. There are times when a person is willing to change, but also times when they are resistant to change. This could be due to various external factors that influence the way they think.

36. c. Shame-attacking is the act of reducing the shame involved with an activity. A is the incorrect answer in that the person in question is not necessarily stopping a behavior so much as that person is trying to adapt to the things that one wishes to do. The person is immersing oneself in the situation and is feeling more confident about their thoughts and behaviors. This includes keeping the fears involved from being intense and ensuring there are no worries about what one might do in the future.

Group Work

1. You notice two people who appear to be communicating with one another in the group you are holding. One of the persons in that group is asking several questions of the other. The person being questioned is starting to feel increasingly uncomfortable. What should you do to control the situation?

    a. Block the person who is asking

    b. Allow the questions to continue

    c. Change the subject

    d. Give the person being questioned the opportunity to respond

2. A member of the group is talking about how he has lost touch with his brother over the years. The leader of the group talks about how they were able to forgive family members who had not been present for much of his life. What is the group counselor illustrating in this situation?

    a. Empathy

    b. Modeling

    c. Transference

    d. Diagnostic effort

3. A person wants to arrange for enough people to conduct a group session. This includes people who have the same interests or have the same objectives and goals. What would the person be called?

    a. Initiator

    b. Harmonizer

    c. Coordinator

    d. None of the above

4. Responsibilities have to be given to each member of the group. These responsibilities may be specific functions or activities within the group. What is the main reason why members would be given these responsibilities?

    a. To keep the group organized

    b. To prevent disobedience

    c. To allow everyone to approve of what is happening

    d. To create a sense of order for who will ask questions first

5. Scapegoats are often found in many situations to blame someone for a particular issue. What would cause people to determine a scapegoat in a situation?

    a. Getting enough facts surrounding the situation

    b. Identifying loose ends or other disconnections in a relationship

    c. Finding a way to resolve a problem as soon as possible

    d. Identifying flaws in the arguments that people have

6. Fear is often produced in groups to make people be worried about what might happen in a situation. What is the overall goal of instilling fear?

    a. Fear helps people understand the problems they need to avoid

    b. Fear causes people to stop complaining about things and to start taking action

    c. Fear is a dramatic effect to make some ideas more memorable or distinct

    d. People could become obsessed about obtaining certain goals

7. What makes reactance distinct in a group setting?

    a. You might react to a situation so that you'll want to engage in some sort of behavior.

    b. You will become vulnerable because you are reacting to a sudden change.

    c. It becomes easier for you to feel more involved.

    d. You may develop an increased sense of resistance to something after being persuaded to agree.

8. People in groups often develop prejudices towards others including those in the same group, by learning more about them. What else can cause a person to develop a prejudice?

    a. General competition

    b. Prior experiences

    c. Aggression

    d. Cognitive thoughts

9. A feminist perspective could be used when conducting a family therapy process. What would be critical to the feminist theory when working with a family's needs?

    a. Identifying who is responsible for dominating the family

    b. Reviewing the roles that each member of the family has

    c. Looking at how the demands for change are imposed on everyone

    d. Deciding the importance of a woman's worth within the family

10. A group therapy session is designed to be confidential, but there might be cases where confidentiality does not have to be kept. Which of these situations would qualify for confidentiality to be broken and for information to be shared?

    a. A person is posting information about the session on social media.

    b. A person is suicidal and could be at risk.

    c. The person has not paid enough money for the services offered.

    d. There are concerns surrounding the quality of a person's relationship With the group.

11. What should the person who conducts a group therapy session talk about with the participants before starting a session?

    a. The risks of any negative outcomes that may develop

    b. Details on the other people who will be in the same group

    c. The activities that you will plan during the session

    d. The amount of effort that the participant should put into the session

12. A support group is a popular type of group for people to learn from others and to be motivated. What is one of the other prominent reason why a support group is useful?

    a. The process is shorter in duration.

    b. People are willing to look at others and judge them for who they are.

    c. People can be aggressive while in a support group.

    d. The focus won't always be on one person.

13. What can be done during an encounter group session?

    a. Anyone can talk about things that might happen in the future.

    b. People can experience intense confrontations with one another.

    c. People will only talk about the concerns they have if they are asked to do so.

    d. All of the above

14. What makes informal learning in a group session distinct in its style?

    a. The learning comes from everyday settings or situations.

    b. A person has the training to decide what can be done in a situation.

    c. A person must follow specific rules to make their actions effective.

    d. Challenges might happen to test one's skills including mock situations.

15. Deindividualization can occur in a group when people suspend their regular identities in a group session. People may start to think about doing things that they might not normally do. What is the main reason why deindividualization may work in a group setting?

    a. To help people understand what others are thinking

    b. To identify the concerns surrounding one's normal behaviors

    c. To be sensitive to the needs of others in a group

    d. All of the above

16. Why is groupthink dangerous?

    a. It causes people to be organized.

    b. People only agree about something for the sake of agreement.

    c. People might be difficult to deal with.

    d. A group can become divided and certain actions might develop as a result.

Answers to Group Work

1. a. A group setting is intended to keep everyone feeling comfortable without feeling judged or rushed in any way. Part of this includes being sensitive to the feelings of others in the group. The leader must block all behaviors that might be undesirable. The most important point is to ensure the person being bothered will have privacy and anything counterproductive will be prevented before the situation becomes difficult to manage.

2. b. Modeling helps a person feel confident about the situation they are in. In this instance, the group leader is talking about the situation and is demonstrating that the person can relate to what another in that group is feeling. Modeling can help identify the positive things that someone should be thinking and doing. This includes producing positive behaviors for someone to emulate.

3. c. The coordinator is the person responsible for bringing people together in a suitable group. A harmonizer is a person who would conduct the session to have everyone work together when the coordinator has formed the group. The initiator is responsible for starting the conversation within the group.

4. b. Disobedience occurs when people are disorganized and no one knows what roles are involved. Disobedience causes people to become frustrated and less likely to be peaceful or in control in a group setting. Deciding the responsibilities of the group members ensure that people will know what they are supposed to do.

5. c. Finding a scapegoat in a group has nothing to do with reason or understanding. Rather, it is about identifying a person to blame. Transferring the blame can cause people to accuse someone and to make quick judgments.

6. a. Fear works when people are aware of the problems. The problems are introduced in a discussion with an explanation as to why the problems are significant. Any warnings could help people understand why a problem has to be resolved before the issue becomes worse.

7. d. Reactance occurs when you might feel a lot of pressure to do something and it is against your normal behavior or against your beliefs. You might choose to deny certain ideas people are promoting due to how you have behaved in the past.

8. a. A competition can directly influence what you are thinking. Aggression is not necessarily a concern unless that aggression has been misplaced and is against the wrong group or individual. Some past actions may also be a factor, although they do not necessarily have been anything you were directly involved with.

9. c. Both the man and woman in the relationship should experience the same changes. That is, neither is expected to be subordinate. A and B would be incorrect in terms of feminist theory, as A is accepting that a man might be in charge of the family and B is considering the roles that people wish to have in a relationship.

10. b. A person who might be at risk of hurting oneself or others should be reported to others in order to protect that person from potential harm or causing harm. The other considerations in this question are more of personal manners, while A focuses on the participant revealing themselves on social media or other avenues.

11. a. It is often easier for people to not know too much about what will happen in a group. The risks involved with what can go wrong should be discussed out of fairness and to produce a sense of understanding over what might develop. Other things that can be discussed include the purpose of therapy, the limits to the confidentiality of the therapy, the possibility for a person to withdraw from the therapy at any time, the possible benefits involved with therapy, and any fees.

12. d. A support group is designed to allow people to work together as a team to resolve certain problems and to improve their thoughts or values. People in the support group will feel comfortable because they are working with others to make positive things happen in their lives and they will have a sense of hope and positivity. The support group helps people who participate to realize that they are not alone as they are trying to resolve the problems they have.

13. b. An encounter group is not designed for people who do not want to share their emotions. It is to help people explore their emotions and to potentially find ways to resolve those feelings. The encounter group can be harsh and confrontational in nature and is not intended for those who might be faint of heart and worried about what might happen during such a session.

14. a. General informal learning does not happen as a result of rigid training or specific lessons. Rather, informal learning involves everyday activities without learning specific courses.

15. b. The practice of deindividualization may help identify problems that people have when trying to behave appropriately. People can use deindividualization to recognize how they might behave by looking at others.

16. b. Groupthink occurs when people are closely linked to one another. Everyone in that group will agree on the same things regardless of how irrational or questionable they might be. The threat is that people might agree on the wrong things and have everyone to agree even if they are wrong or irrational.

Career Development

1. Which of the six main career clusters would represent a position in the field of tourism?

   a. Enterprising

   b. Conventional

   c. Realistic

   d. Social

2. Jordan is working on his Master's degree in business finance so he can work as a manager at a local bank. Which of Super's developmental tasks would Jordan be in at this point?

   a. Crystallization

   b. Stabilization

   c. Implementation

   d. Specification

3. Thomas prefers to take risks with the work that he does. He is very ambitious in his work and feels that you need to work harder if you want to move forward with your work. What type of personality would the Strong Interest Inventory suggest that Thomas has?

   a. Persuader

   b. Doer

   c. Thinker

   d. Creator

4. What can be said about someone who might have an investigative grade in the Holland Code?

    a. The person is an active leader.

    b. Persuasion is critical for that person's work.

    c. There is a strong scientific approach that is used in one's work.

    d. The relationships between many people are critical.

5. What is the focus with the industrial/organizational or I/O psychology concept?

    a. Managing individual behaviors

    b. Reviewing the habits of others and observing how they work

    c. Determining ways to make as much money as possible

    d. Looking at the formalities involved with operating something

6. What is the main goal of human factor psychology in the work environment?

    a. Looking at the human input when developing machines

    b. Identifying the sense of consistency in order to handle the needs of other humans

    c. Planning rules for conduct in the workplace

    d. Producing a simple interface for managing one's work

7. Personnel psychology relates to management that considers organizational efficiency with the proper use of various resources or people. The concept would focus mainly on:

    a. Selecting the right employees

    b. Reviewing how people in the workplace are functioning

    c. Designing jobs that people can complete without risk

    d. All of the above

8. A person who is unsure as to what they want in their career and life after graduating high school is experiencing what kind of crisis?

    a. Self-identity

    b. Vocational identity

    c. Expressive ideas

    d. All of the above

9. An employee performance evaluation can be done at varying times throughout the year to identify how an employee is working. What can go into an evaluation report?

    a. Any possible training someone needs

    b. How much money a person is earning right now

    c. Any ongoing efforts that one might be putting in to complete their work

    d. How often a person comes to work late

10. A job analysis will include a detailed description of which of the following?

    a. The atmosphere that people can expect from the work environment

    b. How much money is paid to the employees

    c. The tasks that someone has to complete

    d. The recruitment process

11. Sexual harassment is a significant threat to various careers. However, there are several problems that happen surrounding sexual harassment and how it is managed. What is the greatest concern in the following list about sexual harassment in the workplace?

    a. Sexual harassment has various definitions that are complicated.

    b. Sexual harassment often goes unreported.

    c. Some reports may be incomplete.

    d. All of the above

12. What is the most common reason why people engage in sexual harassment in the workplace?

    a. To assert power

    b. To satisfy their sexual desires

    c. A person is not thinking about what is happening.

    d. All of the above

13. Equity theory is one of the most prominent theories about how work efforts may be supported and how the working environment is important to employees. Which of the following statements is true about the equity theory?

    a. It is acceptable for people to work longer hours.

    b. A sense of balance is required in how well the business is operating.

    c. People need to feel motivated.

    d. Enough people need to be on hand for a business to stay functional.

14. What is the most common reason why people who are being interviewed for a job might feel worried or anxious?

    a. The situation might be new that person is unaware of the procedure.

    b. The person in the interview doesn't know the person who is conducting the interview.

    c. The person being interviewed is worried they are not qualified for a job.

    d. The person being interviewed knows they're going to be analyzed intensely.

15. What should a person do before a job interview so they can feel comfortable with the interview and less worried?

    a. Research details about the job.

    b. Hold a mock job interview at home.

    c. Try to change your attitudes.

    d. Avoid worrying about the questions that might be asked.

16. According to the social cognitive career theory, what might stop a person from thinking about suitable jobs and careers that might be of interest to them?

    a. Improper self-efficacy thoughts

    b. No background for context

    c. One's general input

    d. All of the above

17. The social cognitive career theory requires people to take a look at many factors about what they can do, including:

    a. Reviewing interests

    b. Identifying the goals one has

    c. Deciding actions that can be taken

    d. All of the above

18. The Archway of Career Determinants involves determining the type of position that might be appropriate for someone. The archway is divided between the biographical and geographical segments. Which of the following will not influence the biographical points in finding a job?

    a. Intelligence

    b. Skillset

    c. Peer groups

    d. Any special interests one has

19. What would Holland say about someone who is realistic in their desire to find work?

    a. The person understands the particular goals required.

    b. The person does not have inflated ideas about what they are capable of.

    c. The person wants to work with tools, machines, and other hands-on materials.

    d. There is a sense of certainty about what one wants to do.

Answers to Career Development

1. d. The work in the hospitality and tourism field is the social career cluster, which focuses on helping other people. This includes working with educational activities, serving the hospitality needs of others, providing general human services, or being protective in the field of law or security. The enterprising field focuses on marketing and sales and with persuasion. Realistic tasks focus on things that have extremely precise controls and standards, including the fields of agriculture and transportation. The conventional field includes information technology or finance.

2. c. Jordan is implementing choosing the position that he wants. He is working on his college degree as he has already specified that he wants to be involved in the financial field. The stabilization process will happen later when he is employed.

3. a. As a persuader, Thomas is a person who is influential and ready to take risks. The strong ambition that Thomas has can also suggest he is a persuader. He may be seen as an enterprising figure. For the other choices, a Doer is someone who is more hands-on and active, but would also think about a more realistic approach to work. A Thinker is someone who is analytical and theoretical and may also pose more questions with the intention of identifying special opportunities for success. A Creator is artistic in nature and is imaginative.

4. c. An investigative person is someone who focuses on scientific and mathematical aspects. The facts are most important for a person in this class. That person is not going to be too aggressive in the work. Also, the investigative person is not someone who would want to lead people or persuade them.

5. a. The I/O concept focuses on individual behaviors and how they are influenced by many factors within a larger organization. A person's behaviors may be impacted by the physical environment of the workplace, the organizational efforts being implemented, and how the work is handled and arranged.

6. a. Human factor psychology is about understanding how machines are developed. All machines are produced to meet the needs of specific people, such as producing unique controls in vehicles or establishing machines that provide automated functions.

7. d. Personnel psychology includes every aspect of a business operation. For instance, the field may focus on what happens before people are employed and distinct job descriptions are developed. The employees must then be chosen correctly and trained to ensure they can handle work. Performance reviews are to

be completed on occasion to identify how the people in the environment are working.

8. b. The vocational identity of a person refers to the things that someone wants to do as employment. The vocational identity is based on a person's interests, goals, skills, and talents.

9. a. A performance evaluation is used to consider the effects of the work one has completed. A review of any possible training that someone might need should be determined. Any praise that someone has earned for one's work and any concerns that might have developed based on the work performed should also be explored in the review process.

10. c. A job analysis focuses on the tasks of a job. These tasks may include a detailed review of the roles that one may accept to complete a task. The job analysis should also look at any processes that link to others in the work. The task can also include the knowledge and abilities needed to complete a job.

11. b. Sexual harassment is often hidden from reports due to factors like a general fear of reprisals. A person might be afraid of being fired from their job due to reporting the incidence of harassment.

12. a. Sexual harassment often occurs because a person wants to exert power over an underling.

13. b. Equity theory is maintaining balance for a business to stay functional. Any imbalances that might occur should be adjusted to allow the workplace to stay functional and to avoid any disputes or other issues that might develop in the workplace. The effort may be loosely related to motivation in that the people in the workplace will feel motivated when there is a sense of balance. Balance can occur regardless of whether there are enough people in the workplace or if some are working more hours than others.

14. d. The general fear that interviewees have is that they're going being analyzed. An interviewee will be tense and worried because they know they will be under scrutiny.

15. b. The best thing to do to get ready for an interview is to plan a role-playing session. The practice can help a person to know what to expect in an interview while considering the answers. Role-playing will lessen the stress of an anticipated interview.

16. a. A person might be prohibited from considering a job because they are not convinced of their ability for the job. As a result, people might ignore possible job

opportunities that they would thrive in because they do not understand themselves or do not recognize their skills and talents.

17. d. The actions that are to be taken follow the goals. Attainments in performance will happen after reviews. Some contextual influences might develop, although these might not be as critical to the development as the self-efficacy and outcome expectations.

18. c. The biological segment entails the needs, values, and interests that a person has. These may be inspired by one's skill sets or interest and possibly the person's personality. The geographical aspects are influences, such as the economy, one's peer groups, the ongoing labor market, social considerations (including family and school influences), and social policies may contribute to the job decision. However, these operate independently from the biographical segment.

19. c. Holland developed six vocational types of people. The realistic segment focuses on people who like to work with their hands. People in the realistic field may work in construction or farming and other jobs where physical effort is required.

Assessment

1. You can provide an essay test to your clients to get open-ended answers surrounding certain concerns that they may have. The answers that you will get should be:

    a. Subjective

    b. Concise

    c. Direct

    d. Objective

2. The difficulty index in an assessment identifies how likely people are to answer a question correctly. Which of the following percentages numbers of the difficulty index suggests that people are more likely to answer correctly?

    a. 25

    b. 34

    c. 45

    d. 55

3. What is the greatest concern of a normative test?

    a. You cannot directly compare the results of one's test with the results that others produced.

    b. The results of the test might be similar to that of other people.

    c. There is a chance that the concept might include personality standards.

    d. Those who have a high IQ will be better at this test.

4. You need to look at how well your test is capable of measuring something that you are intending to measure. What should you consider?

    a. Reliability

    b. Difficulty

    c. Validity

    d. None of the above

5. The reliability of anything you use in the assessment process can help ensure that the results will show which of the following?

    a. Sameness

    b. Random totals

    c. Direct points

    d. Accuracy

6. A spiral test may be conducted to see how a person might respond in a situation. What does this type of test entail?

    a. The test is easier as you go from the start to the end.

    b. There's a variance in difficulty in the content throughout the test.

    c. The content will become more difficult as the test progresses.

    d. There's no standard for the difficulty of the questions.

7. What can you do when aiming to get parallel results of a test that you provide?

    a. Offer a different battery of questions to each person.

    b. Keep the questions the same for everyone.

    c. Allow for one test to be longer than another.

    d. Arrange for one person to have less time than the others to finish the test.

8. A Mental Status Examination or MSE can be conducted to identify which of the following?

   a. One's emotional state

   b. Attitude patterns

   c. Speech habits

   d. All of the above

9. What will a predictive validity of a test show regarding future efforts?

   a. Predict what someone will do

   b. Dictate the course of action a person is to have

   c. Identify a construct for future testing

   d. All of the above

10. You can provide people with the same test in your counseling efforts. This would require that you measure the test results and then compare them with how someone did the first time they took the test. What form of reliability measurement are you working with?

    a. Equal form

    b. Test-retest

    c. Split-half

    d. General analysis

11. Galton conducted a measure of how intelligence is divided among people. What discovery was the result of Galton's work?

    a. Intelligence appears to be normally distributed among people.

    b. People from very specific places or cultures are more intelligent than others.

    c. Some people might have different ideas about what they could do because of their intelligence.

    d. There is a sense of complexity surrounding how intelligence is organized.

12. What makes convergent thinking in an assessment different from divergent thinking?

    a. Convergent thinking will involve different subject matter or processes.

    b. Divergent thinking happens when people from different cultures have unique responses to questions.

    c. Divergent thinking can be complicated and frustrating for people to think about when compared with convergent thinking.

    d. Convergent thinking includes multiple ideas being mixed together.

13. What can be said about the IQ test that Stanford and Binet introduced in the early twentieth century?

    a. It is standardized in nature.

    b. It might only predict certain things that can happen.

    c. This is a non-standardized test.

    d. A and B

14. What is the main point of the IQ test?

    a. To understand how smart someone is

    b. To recognize a person's ability to learn new things

    c. To determine how socially adept a person can be

    d. Whether or not a person has a mental disorder

15. What is the main feature that you will find in a projective test?

    a. A series of neutral details or stimuli

    b. Anything that might reinforce certain thoughts

    c. Emotionally triggering features

    d. Predictive factors

16. What makes an achievement test different from an aptitude test?

    a. An achievement test focuses on potential.

    b. An achievement test focuses on what one has already learned.

    c. An achievement test reviews any unique skills that you might have acquired.

    d. Both tests are the same.

17. You can provide a client with an interest inventory to review how they might respond to certain things or how they might learn a subject. What is the most noticeable in the interest inventory?

    a. A person might try to answer questions according to what they perceive as the most desired response in their society.

    b. A person could offer unique responses based on their personal culture.

    c. There might be many ways to read the questions.

    d. All of the above

18. What does the Buros Mental Measurements Yearbook provide?

    a. Details on psychological tests

    b. Ideas for what to do to produce certain responses

    c. Ideas about where you can go to be tested

    d. How much you should be charging people to take the tests

19. You want to administer a personality factor test to a person of African descent. What should you consider?

    a. Review the details of the test to see if the content is relevant to African people.

    b. Determine if the testing process is suitable based on the beliefs the person has.

    c. Decide how well you understand African culture.

    d. Determine if your client will understand the test.

20. What is the most important thing to note about the results of any test that someone completes?

    a. You need to ensure the test is valid.

    b. The reliability of the test is not very important.

    c. You should not assume that the test is going to be relevant all the time.

    d. This is only one source of information about one's personality or other quality.

Answers to Assessment

1. a. The subjective nature of the essay test suggests that there are no wrong answers. You'd have to review the situation surrounding the person who is providing you with the answer to a question. The full explanation should include enough details about what someone is thinking and why they would answer a question in a particular way.

2. d. The 55% on the difficulty index states that people are 55% likely to get the question correct. In other words, a higher number on the difficulty index means that the question is easier and therefore easier for people to be able to answer correctly.

3. a. A normative test is one where a person's responses are compared with the responses from other people who took the same test. While you might assume that the answers are going to be consistent in some cases, this is not always going to be the case.

4. c. The validity of an assessment refers to how closely the results relate to the content. Although some tests might give you good results, they might not be valid.

5. d. Reliability means that something is consistent and will work in the same way every time. A reliable assessment ensures that you'll get accurate results every time regardless of the participants. Still, you will ensure that the results you are getting are never misleading or confusing.

6. c. The spiral test is one where the difficulty increases as the test progresses. Those who do well in answering earlier questions might have an advantage in understanding the content as it moves forward in the testing process.

7. a. Keeping a unique battery of questions for each person will help you produce parallel answers. In this case, the test entails the same subject matter, but the questions will vary for each person taking the test. The results will not be predictable.

8. d. MSE is one of the most important tests you can conduct. You will measure the MSE based on content such as the emotional state of a person, a person's attitude, the behaviors one exhibit, and any speech patterns or habits that they have. The goal of the MSE is to identify concerns of a person to help you devise a sensible treatment plan.

9. a. Predictive validity is deciding how likely a person is going to do well in future tests or other activities. Academic performance tests like the ACT, SAT, and GRE are all examples of tests that use predictive validity.

10. b. The test-retest method of testing reliability only works when you give the same test to the same person. This includes the same questions and the same rules involved in completing the test. This might work in cases like when you are comparing someone's test before counseling versus the same test after counseling.

11. a. Galton refers to intelligence as a single factor in one's life. The intelligence of people will be divided among people based on who they are and how well they might function in society. In addition, Galton argues that there is a genetic component to intelligence, although it might be difficult to determine the specific genes that will influence one's intelligence.

12. d. Divergent thinking is the process of producing a unique idea in some way. Convergent thinking is looking at how ideas and concepts can develop. Part of this includes finding a way to get the ideas introduced in some form to combined together to create new concepts that include everything as a whole.

13. a. The IQ test that Stanford and Binet devised has a formal procedure and specific standards. Therefore, the test is standardized. However, the test will not predict how well a person might perform in one test, thus the test is not a complete predictor of everything that someone could do.

14. b. The IQ test is designed to figure out how well a person can learn ideas. The test was originally designed to differentiate people who can learn easily from those who cannot in order to divide students into different school classes that fit their specific learning needs.

15. a. The neutral nature of the materials found in the projective test will help identify three important details in a person's mental functions. First, the test will analyze a person's ability to associate certain ideas with others. Second, a test may help decide how well a person can complete certain jobs. The construction segment can require a person to build a new idea or concept from neutral stimuli.

16. a. An achievement test is often given after counseling services are provided. The aptitude test may be offered before counseling. The aptitude test analyzes a person's understanding of the subject matter and estimates the potential for someone to do well in a subject. The achievement test is used to test what someone has already learned.

17. a. Although B and C are sensible considerations, the greatest concern surrounding an interest inventory is that the report might be about a person trying to answer questions according to what is socially acceptable. Someone might change their answers in the hopes of not being judged by other people.

18. a. The Buros Mental Measurements Yearbook has been providing help to counselors and psychological experts to find testing processes since Oscar Buros first produced the book in 1938. The book has been consistently updated with details on how to complete tests.

19. c. One's culture might directly influence the way someone might respond to questions. Customs might directly influence a person's answers and their understanding of the questions.

20. d. The results of one test should not be considered the final determination of how a person will act or behave. A and B are not correct because reliability is much more important to your test than the validity.

Research and Program Evaluation

1. The Hawthorne effect may be used in some research to identify how well someone is performing versus anything that is contributed to the test. What would happen when the Hawthorne effect is used?

    a. People might feel that they are doing better after consuming something even though what was just consumed is useless.

    b. A trait that no one is trying to measure will influence a trait that is being actively measured.

    c. The beliefs that you might have may prompt you to get people to act differently because you want certain results.

    d. People will change their behaviors because they know that someone is watching.

2. What makes a cross-sectional study different from a longitudinal one?

    a. The timeframe involved

    b. The results you wish to find

    c. How people might respond to certain stimuli

    d. All of the above

3. You are trying to gather as many people for a counseling study as possible, but you are struggling. You have certain parameters involved choose certain participants, but you are not getting enough people in each of the groups you wish to work with. What form of sampling would be recommended at this point?

    a. Random

    b. Quota

    c. Cluster

    d. Standardized

4. You want to analyze the variables in a test by using a chart to illustrate how the work is being handed. What will you use on the X-axis on your chart?

   a. Dependent variable

   b. Independent variable

   c. A timeframe for how long you are measuring things for

   d. B and C

5. What is the best way for a hypothesis to be explained in your studies?

   a. You are reviewing general rules or laws to see what might happen.

   b. You are trying to support something with a statement of your own.

   c. You are exaggerating something.

   d. You are making an educated guess about conclusions.

6. What makes an alternative hypothesis different from a regular hypothesis?

   a. The alternative hypothesis will be false.

   b. An alternative hypothesis will state what you actually expect.

   c. You are stating a distinct theory with your hypothesis

   d. The new hypothesis might be flexible and could change, unlike a regular hypothesis that might not change.

7. What makes a naturalistic observation unique for a test?

   a. You are reviewing something in its native environment.

   b. You are analyzing how a unique variable may be included.

   c. You will ask people questions about the things that are changing.

   d. No variables are being incorporated in the testing process.

8. What makes a case study different from other tests that you might use in research?

    a. A case study focuses on only one item.

    b. You are looking at specific techniques that might develop.

    c. The analysis might produce broad ideas of what can happen.

    d. There's no real difference between a case study and any other test.

9. You are trying to analyze the concerns of a person who has recently served overseas. You are noticing general worries from that person surrounding the events one is in right now and how that person thinks about them. What could you do to plan a program for that person?

    a. Determine the symptoms that the person displays.

    b. Find a treatment plan that would be appropriate.

    c. Analyze the sample group that the person can join.

    d. Ask about medications that might be effective.

10. A meta-analysis can be conducted to help you identify possible changes or actions that might occur. What could help you identify the results of a meta-analysis review?

    a. Feedback from the subjects in your study

    b. Peer support

    c. Research content

    d. The studies that you've reviewed

11. Participant observation is somewhat related to natural observation. What does a participant observation practice involve?

    a. You add various other people into the natural site including many who might clash with the others who are native to the area.

    b. You can review everything the people are doing in as many rooms as possible.

    c. The researcher joins in and interacts with the people involved.

    d. All of the above

12. You can choose to conduct a correlational review of information in a quantitative research study. What is the main goal of a quantitative study?

    a. Observing things that can happen

    b. Finding relationships between many variables

    c. Reviewing the causality

    d. Identifying the ways variables might be changed and how impacts might occur in the process

13. Cohort effects will involve the following:

    a. How many people within one group might try to be as identical to one another as possible

    b. How smart people might be in the studies and how they are going to respond to activities

    c. Any changes that might occur in the study

    d. Things happening to people based on their historical experiences

14. Causal research can help you identify:

  a. The potential for one variable to be the reason why another variable is changing

  b. A specific description of whatever is happening at a time

  c. How variables are related to one another

  d. All of the above

15. What is the general approach that people use to find information on certain situations or activities that might develop in the workplace or another environment?

  a. Systematic method

  b. Hypothetical approach

  c. General analysis

  d. Scientific method

16. For what period of time should you analyze the quality of the test answers?

  a. Based on past events

  b. Based on future potential

  c. Based on what is happening right now

  d. At any point depending on what you feel is appropriate

Answers to Research and Program Evaluation

1. d. The Hawthorne effect can be noticed when you add security cameras or you change the general monitoring effects in the workplace. People know that they are being watched, thus causing them to act differently. A is the placebo effect used in tests that entail drug use or treatments. B is the halo effect and focuses on certain actions that change while looking at other actions. C is the Rosenthal effect and is relative to the expectations that the experimenter might have regarding the testing process or the subject matter.

2. a. The cross-sectional study format includes many people who are in different segments of a population. These include people in different groups based on age, gender, location, or income. A longitudinal study would use the same grouping of people being reviewed during an extended time period.

3. c. Cluster sampling entails working with people within certain segments of a population chosen at one time. A quota sampling is the opposite in that you are only choosing very specific people for the test. Random sampling is choosing participants at random without specifying specifics.

4. d. You can work with an independent variable on the X-axis if you are changing a particular variable and looking to see how the dependent variable changes. The dependent variable will be measured on the Y-axis. Time may also be used as a consideration if you plan on observing how the results can change over an extended period.

5. d. The hypothesis is an educated guess of the results of the study. The hypothesis might be proven true or untrue.

6. b. The alternative hypothesis considers the real expectations that you have for some event. You may use this type of hypothesis to go against a null hypothesis of an earlier study. You will accept the alternative hypothesis if the earlier null hypothesis was not acceptable.

7. a. The most important part of the naturalistic observation process is that you are analyzing a group in its own environment. For instance, you might observe children at a school and see how well they behave and how they respond to different activities taking place all around. The testing is not necessarily reflective of any variables that you might add.

8. a. You will concentrate on a single subject in your case study. This may be one person or maybe a small group of the population of people who are being supported.

9. a. The best way to plan is to consider the symptoms someone is expressing. You might also have to move the person to a unique testing process based on those symptoms.

10. c. You can use various research content to identify how your methods compare to different concepts you wish to support. It is beneficial to analyze the quality of the study based on the literature that you have. The meta-analysis lets you decide if your plan is sensible and useful for your study.

11. c. Participant observation is observing the people in your group and how they work so that you can potentially observe some new perspectives about what the people in a situation are doing. You may need to be covert when recording things or acknowledging that you are a part of the study so that the people you are observing do not change their behaviors.

12. b. The correlational study is a review of the relationships between variables. This may involve a review of the relationship between stress in life and the risk of depression. A refers to a descriptive quantitative study that involves looking at something that happens when the variables are not controlled. C is the quasi-experimental study that involves the review of a situation and the causality without an independent variable is changed. D is an experimental process where you will adjust the independent variable and see how the changes might make certain things happen.

13. d. The cohorts in this situation are people who are similar. These include people who work in the same department or are the same age among other factors. The cohort effects are things that come about due to the influences that these people have on each other.

14. a. Causal research involves looking at how certain variables work based on the results that may be triggered. A research process can involve looking at the cause and effect of a situation. You can use this to change variables while determining the causes that might be influenced.

15. d. The scientific method is the root of all studies. It involves collecting data, stating a hypothesis, and coming to conclusions that either proves the hypothesis true or untrue.

16. d. You will have to look at the particular time that your test is questioning. You can look at immediate occurrences, or prior events to determine what might have caused things to happen or predict something that may happen in the future based on what you are reviewing.

Orientation and Ethics

1. What type of client relationship is not allowed?

    a. A relationship where you have been providing counseling to a person who is in the same family

    b. If you have provided services to them in the past and they are starting to see you again.

    c. A relationship where they are providing another service to you

    d. All of the above

2. There might be times when a clinical office with many counselors has multiple clients who need services. What can be considered to decide where clients should be placed and which counselors should see them?

    a. How many cases the counselor is dealing with right now

    b. Demographic details about the case

    c. The expertise that a counselor has

    d. All of the above

3. A community needs assessment may be conducted to identify the needs that a community has for counseling services. This includes looking at the ongoing well-being of people in the local area. What should your analysis of the area include?

    a. Details about hospitalizations for certain conditions

    b. School attendance rates

    c. Amount of money people earn every year

    d. All of the above

4. You have the option to consistently monitor your clients based on how they are progressing with counseling. What should your notes include?

    a. How often people are getting into trouble

    b. The willingness of a person to move forward with treatment

    c. Any risks that someone might encounter during the treatment process

    d. All of the above

5. Ruling 42 CFR Part II ensures that data about drug and alcohol patients are kept confidential and secure. What is the main reason why this process is to be used in the work environment?

    a. To ensure that people receive the help they need

    b. To encourage people to get help

    c. To identify possible medications in the treatment

    d. So counselors can decide people they would easily serve and support

6. You might be experienced with cognitive behavior therapy, but a client is interested in another avenue of support. What should you do in this case?

    a. Decline to offer this to the client

    b. Bring in someone from outside the office to help you

    c. Refer that person to someone who understands what that person wants

    d. Provide help with that alternative concept within your scope of understanding

7. You have just recently spoken to your client about their next appointment. Someone you know is asking about your client. What is the best possible way for you to respond to the query?

    a. Ignore the person altogether

    b. State that you are not allowed to speak about the situation

    c. Mention that the client has plenty of issues

    d. Talk about as many things as you wish within reason

8. A release of information document may be provided to your client to identify things that might be happening during your counseling sessions. What can be said about a release of information document?

    a. It may only work for a limited time.

    b. There are still limits as to what you can say.

    c. The client has to agree to the information in the document.

    d. All of the above

9. You are contemplating accept payment through insurance policies owned by some of your clients. First you must confirm that you are capable of offering services depending on the clients' diagnoses. What should you reference to confirm a person's diagnosis so that their insurance policy can be accepted?

    a. PDR

    b. DSM

    c. APA

    d. NBCC

10. Although online counseling services might be valuable, it is strongly recommended that you avoid providing online help. What is the main reason it would be difficult or impractical to offer online services?

   a. Not everyone is capable of having access to online services.

   b. You might experience time restrictions for your appointments.

   c. The technical limitations involved with online services could make it difficult for you to reach people and stay connected.

   d. You can only serve people in whatever state you are licensed to be a counselor.

11. Quality assurance is needed to ensure your counseling is done with care and accuracy. What does quality assurance entail?

   a. Keeping files on your clients up-to-date

   b. Arranging your office layout

   c. Keeping the air on in your office

   d. All of the above

12. You are working with another counselor and you want to determine if the arrangement is effective. You want to review how that counselor is handling meetings with clients. What should you do before monitoring another counselor's work?

   a. Ask the client for permission

   b. Review where you are going to keep a hidden camera secure

   c. Ask a client about what they think

   d. A and B

13. You want to educate people in your counseling clinic about diversity and cultural awareness. How would you do this?

    a. Explain the geographic locations of people

    b. Discuss various beliefs that people have

    c. Analyzing one's attitudes regarding counseling

    d. All of the above

14. You are in a situation where you need to refer a client to another party for further review or to provide analysis about something you are not familiar with. What do you need to do?

    a. Allow the client to go to a third party without limitations.

    b. Give the client a listing of options for a referral.

    c. Provide the appropriate referral data of the client to the third party.

    d. Ask the client if they need a referral.

15. A clinical supervisor will be hired to assist you with counseling clients. You would have to talk with the clinical supervisor regularly. How often should you communicate with the supervisor?

    a. Every week

    b. Every month

    c. Two to three times a year

    d. Varies by state

16. A counselor of Middle Eastern descent is going to work alongside a counselor of Maori descent. What would be the best thing for the first counselor to do?

   a. Diversity training

   b. Further studies in Maori culture

   c. Be transferred to a different place

   d. Nothing is required

17. You are looking through a report but the content in that report is obsolete. A newer version of the report is available, or there is some data in another report that should be included. What should you do with the obsolete report?

   a. Keep notes on what data is obsolete.

   b. Avoid using the old report.

   c. Compare the old report with the new one to identify any changes.

   d. Keep working with your report as planned.

18. Bartering is often provided as a solution to pay for services in some parts of the world. In bartering, a person would accept goods or services in exchange for a different product or service. Should you consider bartering in exchange for counseling services?

   a. It depends on what you are getting in return.

   b. Always use bartering if you can.

   c. Avoid bartering at all times.

   d. Check your local board to see what the standards for bartering are.

19. What does it mean to provide your services pro bono publico?

    a. Services are offered free of charge

    b. Reduced fees are offered.

    c. You would only be allowed to work in one particular field of specialty.

    d. A and B

20. Some of the records that you will keep are ones that are based on an artistic nature. What does this concept mean?

    a. Your client has created something during counseling.

    b. You are establishing new ideas of what someone can do during a session.

    c. You are bringing more people into a session to expand what can be done.

    d. You are being more flexible about things you wish to talk about with your client.

21. Sexual harassment is illegal in the counseling environment. What would a situation that is considered sexual harassment entail?

    a. Entail nothing that people will remember

    b. Could be something that people might laugh about later

    c. Cause the work environment to become hostile

    d. Create an imbalance of men and women in the work environment

22. Although a minor usually requires the approval of their parents or legal guardians to receive counseling services, there are times when the minor might be capable of requesting help on their own. When can a minor agree to receive counseling services without having to ask an adult for permission?

   a. If the minor has enough money to pay for the service

   b. If the adults caring for the minor are unable to make decisions

   c. If there are no adults in the minor's life

   d. The rules vary according to the jurisdiction

23. What should you do to prepare a social media site for your counseling services?

   a. Provide details on how your services are helping individual clients

   b. Offer videos of any services that you have conducted in the past

   c. Ask people for details on what you can do to improve your services

   d. Keep your counseling services separate from what is on your personal page

24. What should you not list on your counseling services website?

   a. Specific procedures that you wish to undertake

   b. The benefits of what you have to offer

   c. Any limits over what you can do

   d. How counseling services work and what that service is unable to accomplish

25. What ethical considerations exist about the use of the existential theory when counseling people?

   a. Everyone has unique reasons why they are doing things in their lives.

   b. It might be difficult to explain rational activities as the world continues to change.

   c. Your client might not be fully aware of how the theory works.

   d. Some people might refuse to listen to ideas that they think are pretentious.

26. Although you can incorporate many of Freud's theories in your counseling, his work is still debatable based on ethical considerations. What is the main concern about Freud's theories?

   a. The basis of belief for his theory is very sensible but can be complicated.

   b. Much of his theories require identifying conscious thoughts.

   c. Freud's theories are based on individual studies and do not include definitions for how normal people behave.

   d. All of the above

27. You are planning a test in your counseling firm and you need to find enough people to participate. What do you need from the clients before you administer the test?

   a. Informed consent

   b. Payment

   c. A review of one's results

   d. A promise not to tell anyone about the test

28. Some people that you analyze in a counseling setting might not have the mental capacity to understand what you are discussing. What is the best thing for you to do in this situation?

    a. Allow an assistant who works with that person to attend your session.

    b. Have an independent assistant who can work with the challenged attend the session.

    c. Provide written documentation or other things that might be easy for the person to understand.

    d. Have the parents or guardians of the person you are counseling attend the session too.

29. Is it ever acceptable for you to discuss concerns surrounding the counseling of your client with other members of their family? (Note: This question relates to taking care of adult patients.)

    a. Yes

    b. No

    c. Voice your concerns only with the immediate family members.

    d. This varies by state.

Answers to Orientation and Ethics

1. c. You are not allowed to provide services to anyone with whom you have a concurrent relationship. For example, you cannot provide counseling to someone who is also your lawyer. A relationship such as this is a dual relationship. You cannot provide services to someone with whom you have or have had a romantic relationship. This is not ethical due to the influence that can occur surrounding other services that are being provided. You are allowed to counsel a person who might have had an extended gap between services with you.

2. d. Each of the factors is appropriate in that clients need to be assigned to counselors who are more likely to provide care. For A, a person who has too many clients or cases at a time might not be able to provide the appropriate amount of support for a client. For B, there might be times when a person might prefer to work with someone who is of the same demographics. This does not mean an office needs to refer people based on demographics. C is also sensible in that the suggestions and advice from a doctor with expertise might be more easily accepted by certain clients.

3. a. You can get information on hospitalization through your report. This includes an analysis of major hospitals in your area as well as any mental health or rehabilitation services. You can review the statistics of treatment places to decide what approaches would be more effective. You may also explore trends that might indicate what types of services might be required now or possibly in the future.

4. d. You could plan an analysis of how many risks a client is encountering in their life based on reports of the client's progress. You can determine if your clients are comfortable or not. This includes giving your client enough support for many activities you suggest.

5. b. Rule 42 CFR Part II concerns reducing the fear of hiring a counseling service. Many people worry that they will have their activities reported to the other authorities. Rule 42 CFR Part II ensures that counselors cannot report details unless the client appears to be at risk of harming themselves or other people. Also, a client must provide a counselor with permission to allow details of their counseling session to be given to someone else.

6. d. This involves protecting a relationship with a client. However, you must provide details on your scope of practice so your client will understand what services you are able to provide. The other answers are incorrect.

7. b. A could technically be correct, but the best thing to do is B - you cannot disclose information about a client's situation. Ethical standards state that you should not divulge any information about a client unless you have the client's permission to do so.

8. d. A release of information document must be approved by your client. The document states that you can release certain information to other parties. Those details should be limited in scope and explicitly described in the document. The release of information has a time restraint that is agreed to by the counselor and the client.

9. b. The DSM is the Diagnostic and Statistical Manual of Mental Disorders. The guide is an official reference to identify mental conditions and how they might evolve. This is used by the APA or American Psychiatric Association to identify what patients are suffering from to manage insurance policy claims. The PDR is incorrect as the Physicians' Desk Reference refers to prescription drugs and how they are to be prescribed. The NBCC is the organization that operates the NCE test to certify counselors.

10. d. You need to register for the exam in your particular part of the country. This includes registering based on certain accreditation standards that may apply in your area. It could be unlawful to counsel people from outside your state while online. However, you may be allowed to help people outside your state depending on where you are located. You'll have to ask your certification board for details of what you can and cannot do.

11. a. Quality assurance refers to ensuring that the client's records are detailed and up-to-date. All the documents on your client should be filled out accordingly and should be updated based on the most recent developments and visits regarding your client as well as details on their progress should be noted.

12. a. You need to ask the client about the possibility of filming or sitting in on the session. This is to ensure the client will not feel uncomfortable with what is planned to happen. You should not use a hidden camera, as it might create a sense of fear. Asking a client about what they think about a counselor is not appropriate.

13. b. Training your employees in diversity requires considering many concerns about how people might behave. You will have to consider how people in various countries develop according to their culture.

14. c. You should provide information about the client to the referral agency so the client can be supported by the counselor.

15. d. When your supervisor is to meet with you will vary based on the state you are in. You need to check with the licensing division in your area. In most cases, you might see a supervisor every month, although the rules may be different based on the state you are in.

16. a. Diversity training helps people learn more about the people that they are going to work with or serve. You can use diversity training to understand more about cultures that you might not be fully aware of. This eases communication between counselor and client so that they both can communicate with each other with understanding.

17. b. You should use the newer report. You might also have to switch to another reporting standard based on whether or not the content in the newer report is relevant to the present work. You should avoid comparing reports. The old report might be obsolete for various reasons such as the content in question no longer being valuable for your study.

18. c. It is difficult to decide the value of counseling services when bartering is considered. You should not risk engaging in any unusual situations or relationships with your clients.

19. d. You have the option to work for free or with reduced fees when you operate pro bono publico. The concept means that you are providing counseling services to society and will provide a portion of your services free of charge. This may be applicable if you want to offer services to non-profit organizations or if you want to work for low-income clients who might not normally afford standard services. You may also use this concept when you speak to larger groups of people.

20. a. Records of an artistic nature are what a client has created during a session. Such records may be collected and analyzed to review the emotional or mental status of a client. For instance, a person might be asked to draw a picture of something that happened. This can help you to gauge the progress that your client is making.

21. c. Acts of sexual harassment can encompass calling people names, touching them in the wrong places, or trying to get too close to them. Encouraging sexual activities may also be a concern. These acts might be difficult for people to forget and will create a hostile environment.

22. d. Every state has rules regarding when a minor can legally seek counseling. In most cases, this might be due to the legal parents or guardians in one's life not being available or those people not being responsible. Cases where the minor's

life could be at risk may also suggest someone requires counseling. You would have to check your state's rules regarding services.

23. d. Ethical standards state that you need to keep your personal social media activities separate from your professional ones. Fortunately, many social media outlets will allow you to produce a secondary page for your professional activities.

24. a. You should not discuss things that you can do for others on your site. You need to ensure the details involved with what you want to do are not exposed. Rather, you should talk about the positives or your services. You must also mention that there are limits as to what you can do and that there are certain things that you cannot do or accomplish. You should also mention that there are many rules for how a counsel operates.

25. b. Existential theory considers how a person attempts to make rational decisions even when the situation is irrational. Much of this is dedicated to the meaning of life. The practice can be frustrating for many to predict behavior.

26. c. Much of the work that Freud completed was based on individual studies. Many of Freud's ideas are based on unconscious thoughts that may influence a person's thought process and actions.

27. a. The ethical solution to use in your experimentation is to ask for informed consent. A person will receive the appropriate information surrounding a test before they agree to participate. The information should be given to allow the participant to decide on whether or not they want to partake in the study. A participant should not pay you, although you could pay them for being in the study.

28. b. The best thing to do is to invite an independent assistant to attend your session rather than someone the client regularly meets with. An independent party will ensure that the information being provided to your client is delivered by a neutral body without issues of understanding developing. You should ensure that the person who is going to help your client through the process understands your plan and understands the client.

29. b. You should not try to communicate with other family members of your client. You need to ensure that your client understands the treatment process and that their information will be protected. This includes not telling any other person about whatever is happening in your sessions with your client. It will still be acceptable to share information with your client's family if your client appears to be a threat to their own mental health.

Conclusion

The details encompassed by the NCE test are important for you to know. You need to notice what you can do when completing the test and that you have a sensible idea of what you will get out of the testing process. Each of the eight segments of the test is extensive and will challenge your knowledge of counseling.

Good luck in your efforts in completing the NCE test. You will find that you can succeed quite well if you review all the segments of the test.

Made in the USA
Middletown, DE
22 November 2019